CLASSIC HYMNS

CLASSIC
HYMNS

General Editor: Lore Ferguson Wilbert

NASHVILLE, TENNESSEE

Published by B&H Publishing Group
Nashville, Tennessee

Dewey Decimal Classification: 264.23
Subject Heading: HYMNS \ CHURCH MUSIC \
RELIGIOUS POETRY

Unless otherwise noted, all Scripture quotations are taken
from the King James Version. Public domain.

1 2 3 4 5 6 7 • 21 20 19 18 17

Contents

———— ✤ ————

Letter to the Reader

———— ✦ ————

Traditional. Contemporary. Alternative. Country. Large band. No instruments. Arms up. Still. Dancing in the aisles. Every person has their own preference and style when it to comes to worship. Is one more spiritual than another? Is one way of singing more pleasing to God's ear? No, worship is the outward expression of the hearts pulling towards God, and not a competition. It is not the style that is important. But if that is true- what is important?

Sometimes it can become easy to get lost in the emotion and passion of worship. In worshipping through song, we praise the Lord not only with our joyful noise, but with our words. Have you ever sat down and thought through the words you were singing? Have you ever thought through the biblical backing of your declarations?

Through the singing of classic hymns we get the opportunity to both praise the God of the universe, and connect with the great cloud of witnesses that have come before us by singing the same words that have been used for generations.

While soaking in these hymns I was struck with the instant connection I felt to the Church. And not the local congregation, but all Christians across all time. The men and women who wrote these hymns felt the same longing in 1600 as I feel today; the same adoration that I melt into in a service, and the same need to confess their sins. I pray as you journey through these pages you feel the same connection to those who surround you, and have come before you.

If you have ever read lyrics to a song before, you know that sometimes lyrists like to get creative with their spelling, grammar, punctuation, and occasionally even make up a few words. All of this was kept as close to the original form as possible to hold onto the poetic nature of the songs.

A final piece of advice for the reflection you are about to begin. Read each song multiple times. Read it as a song. Read it as a poem. Read it as a letter. Sing it out loud! Allow the words of the hymn to flow out of you, so that as you reflect on their meaning, they become your prayers to the Lord.

1. Holy, Holy, Holy

———— ✠ ————

Words: Reginald Heber 1783–1826
Music: John B. Dykes, 1823–1876

Holy, holy, holy! Lord God almighty! Early in the morning our song shall rise to Thee; Holy, holy, holy, merciful and mighty! God in three Persons, blessed Trinity!

Holy, holy, holy! all the saints adore Thee, Casting down their golden crowns around the glassy sea; Cherubim and seraphim falling down before Thee, Who wert, and art, and evermore shalt be.

Holy, holy, holy! tho' the darkness hide Thee, Tho' the eye of sinful man Thy glory may not see; Only Thou art holy; there is none beside Thee, Perfect in pow'r, in love, and purity.

Holy, holy, holy! Lord God Almighty! All Thy works shall praise Thy name, in earth, and sky, and sea; Holy, holy, holy! merciful and mighty! God in three Persons, blessed Trinity!

Bible Study Questions

1. Read Isaiah 6.
2. What does this passage say about God and His character?
3. What does this passage say about Isaiah, and man in general?

Personal Reflection Questions

1. Think of a time when you were undone by the majesty of God.
2. Did this experience change you in any way?
3. How does knowing the character of God change you in the monotony of your normal days?

Prayer

Pray a prayer of worship and adoration to God, praising Him for His character and majesty.

2. To God Be the Glory

———— ✠ ————

Words: Fanny J. Crosby, 1820–1915
Music William H. Doane, 1832–1915

To God be the glory, great things He hath done; So loved He the world that He gave His Son, who yielded His life an atonement for sin, And opened the lifegate that all may go in.

Praise the Lord, praise the Lord, Let the earth hear His voice! Praise the Lord, praise the Lord, Let the people rejoice! O come to the Father, thro' Jesus the Son, And give Him the glory, great things He hath done.

O perfect redemption, the purchase of blood, To ev'ry believer the promise of God; The vilest offender who truly believes, That moment from Jesus a pardon receives.

Praise the Lord, praise the Lord, Let the earth hear His voice! Praise the Lord, praise the Lord, Let the people rejoice! O come to the Father, thro' Jesus the Son, And give Him the glory, great things He hath done.

Great things He hath taught us, great things He hath done, And great our rejoicing thro' Jesus the Son; But purer, and higher, and greater will be Our wonder, our vict'ry, when Jesus we see.

Praise the Lord, praise the Lord, Let the earth hear His voice! Praise the Lord, praise the Lord, Let the people rejoice! O come to the Father, thro' Jesus the Son, And give Him the glory, great things He hath done.

Bible Study Questions

1. Read John 14:1–14.
2. What might have seemed confusing to the disciples in this conversation?
3. Why was it important to convey that no one comes to the Father except through the Son?

Personal Reflection Questions

1. Is it easier for you to relate to the Father or the Son? Why?
2. What is meant in this hymn by "perfect redemption"?

3. Does your redemption seem "perfect"? Why or why not?

4. What does the Bible say about the redemption of those who come to Christ?

Prayer

Pray a prayer of thanksgiving, praising God for all the ways He expresses Himself in His Word for your redemption.

3. All People That on Earth Do Dwell

———— ✠ ————

Words: Paraphrased, William Kethe 1594; Thomas Ken,
   1637–1711
Music: *Genevan Psalter*, 1551 Edition; attr. Louis Bougeois,
   1510–1561

All people that on earth do dwell, Sing to the Lord with cheerful voice; Him serve with fear, His praise forth-tell; Come ye before Him an rejoice.

The Lord, ye know is God indeed, Without our aid He did us make; We are His folk, He doth us feed, And for His sheep He doth us take.

O enter then His gates with praise, Approach with joy His courts unto; Praise laud, and bless His name always, For it is seemly so to do.

*For why? the Lord our God is good, His mercy is forever sure;
His truth at all times firmly stood, And shall from age to age
endure.*

*Praise God, from whom all blessings flow; Praise Him, all
creatures here below; Praise Him above, yes heav'nly host;
Praise Father, Son, and Holy Ghost.*

Bible Study Questions

1. Read Psalm 100.
2. What would "come before his presence" (v. 2) have
   meant to the earliest listeners of this psalm, since
   Christ had not yet come and fulfilled the law?

Personal Reflection Questions

1. What are some actions that prepare your heart for
   worship, prayer, and communion with God?
2. Do you feel you have to do something in order to
   dwell with God? To enter His presence?
3. How does the knowledge that you are His change
   how you enter His presence?

Prayer

Pray a prayer thanking God that He has made a way to dwell with Him and for sending His Spirit to be with you always.

4. Immortal, Invisible God Only Wise

———— ❖ ————

Words: Walter Chalmers Smith, 1824–1908
Music: Welsh Hymn Tune

Immortal, invisible, God only wise, In light inaccessible hid from our eyes, Most blessed, most glorious, the Ancient of Days, Almighty, victorious, Thy great name we praise.

Unresting, unhasting, and silent as light, Nor wanting, nor wasting, Thou rulest in might; Thy justice, like mountains, high soaring above Thy clouds, which are fountains of goodness and love.

To all, life Thou givest, to both great and small; In all life Thou livest, the true life of all; We blossom and flourish as leaves on the tree, And wither and perish—but naught changeth Thee.

Great Father of glory, pure Father of light, Thine angels adore Thee, all veiling their sight; All praise we would render; O help us to see 'Tis only the splendor of light hideth Thee!

Bible Study Questions

1. Read James 1:16–18.
2. What is meant by the "Father of lights"? How might the early listeners have understood this passage?

Personal Reflection Questions

1. Which three aspects of God's character in this song are most difficult for you to believe about Him?
2. List the ways in which God has been faithful to display these characteristics to you.

Prayer

Pray a prayer of confession for not trusting the Father to supply all your needs and praise Him for His unchangeableness (Hebrews 6:17–20).

5. Joyful, Joyful, We Adore Thee

————— ✢ —————

Words: Henry van Dyke, 1852–1933
Music: Ludwig van Beethoven 1770–1827

*Joyful, joyful, we adore Thee, God of glory, Lord of love;
Hearts unfold like flow'rs before Thee, Op'ning to the sun
above. Melt the clouds of sin and sadness; Drive the dark of
doubt away; Giver of immortal gladness, Fill us with the light
of day!*

*All Thy works with job surround Thee, Earth and heav'n
reflect Thy rays, Stars and angels sing around Thee, Center of
unbroken praise. Field and forest, vale and mountain, Flow'ry
meadow, flashing sea, Singing bird and flowing fountain Call
us to rejoice in Thee.*

*Thou art giving and forgiving, Ever blessing, ever blest, Well-
spring of the joy of living, Ocean-depth of happy rest! Thou
our Father, Christ our Brother—All who live in love are Thine;
Teach us how to love each other, Lift us to the joy divine.*

Bible Study Questions

1. Read Philippians 4:1–9.
2. What situation is Paul admonishing the Philippians to respond to in this passage?
3. How does the presence of joy change our response to conflict or hardship?

Personal Reflection Questions

1. "Clouds of sin and sadness", "dark of doubt", and "broken praise:": what in your life today feels wrought with these realities?
2. When you find joy in the midst of these realities, what is its source?
3. Write the promises in this hymn to those whose joy is in Christ.

Prayer

Pray a prayer of supplication, asking the Father to bring you joy in the midst of today's challenges and sufferings.

6. A Mighty Fortress Is Our God

———— ✠ ————

Words: Martin Luther, 1483–1546; tr. Frederic H. Hedge,
      1805–1890
Music: Martin Luther

A mighty fortress is our God, A bulwark never failing; Our helper He, amid the flood Of mortal ills prevailing: For still our ancient foe Doth seek to work us woe; His craft and pow'r are great, And, armed with cruel hate, On earth is not his equal.

Did we in our own strength confide, Our striving would be losing; Were not the right Man on our side, The Man of God's own choosing: Dost ask who that may be? Christ Jesus, it is He; Lord Sabbaoth, His name From age to age the same, And He must win the battle.

And tho' this world, with devils filled, Should threaten to undo us, We will not fear, for God hath willed His truth to triumph thro' us: The Prince of Darkness grim, We tremble not for him; His rage we can endure, For lo, his doom is sure, One little word shall fell him.

That word above all earthly pow'rs, No thanks to them, abideth; The Spirit and the gifts are ours Thro' Him who with us sideth: Let goods and kindred go, This mortal life also; The body they may kill: God's truth abideth still, His kingdom is forever.

Bible Study Questions

1. Read John 10:1–18.
2. List out what this passage says about the thief, wolves, hired hands, strangers, and robbers.
3. List out what this passage says about the good shepherd, the sheep, the gatekeeper, the Father, and the flock.
4. What might each of these things represent?

Personal Reflection Questions

1. How does the truth of who the Good Shepherd is change how you regard what you are afraid of?
2. What is there to fear?

3. How do this passage and this hymn speak directly to your fears?

Prayer

Pray a prayer of confession in regard to your fears, asking God to calm them and remove them, and then worship Him for His faithfulness.

7. From All That Dwells Below the Skies

———— ✠ ————

Words: Isaac Watts, 1674–1748
Music: John Hatton, c. 1710–1793

From all that dwell below the skies, Let the Creator's praise arise; Let the Redeemer's name be sung, Thro' ev'ry land by ev'ry tongue.

Eternal are Thy mercies, Lord; Eternal truth attends Thy word; Thy praise shall sound from shore to shore, Till suns shall rise and set no more.

Bible Study Questions

1. Read Revelation 7.
2. What is meant by the word *sealed* in verses 4–8?

Personal Reflection Questions

1. How does the knowledge that the children of God are sealed bring you joy today?
2. What does being "sealed" mean for your life? What does it not mean?

Prayer

Spend some time thanking and praising God for inviting you into His kingdom and for sealing you as His.

8. Come, Thou Fount of Every Blessing

———— ✠ ————

Words: Robert Robinson, 1735–1790
Music: *Wyeth's Repository of Sacred Music, Part Second,* 1813

Come Thou Fount of ev'ry blessing, Tune my heart to sing Thy grace; Streams of mercy, never ceasing, Call for songs of loudest praise: Teach me some melodious sonnet, Sung by flaming tongues above; Praise the mount! I'm fixed upon it, Mount of Thy redeeming love.

Here I raise mine Ebenezer; Hither by Thy help I'm come; And I hope, by Thy good pleasure, Safely to arrive at home: Jesus sought me when a stranger, Wand'ring from the fold of God; He, to rescue me from danger, Interposed His precious blood.

O to grace how great a debtor Daily I'm constrained to be! Let Thy grace, Lord, like a fetter, Bind my wand'ring heart to Thee: Prone to wander, Lord, I feel it, Prone to leave the God I love; Here's my heart, Lord, take and seal it, Seal it for Thy courts above.

Bible Study Questions

1. Read 1 Samuel 7:3–14.
2. What was the significance of naming the stone "Hitherto hath the LORD helped us" (v. 12)?
3. Were the people of Israel at the end of their suffering at this point?

Personal Reflection Questions

1. Think of a time when God proved Himself faithful to you in an astounding way. Did it help assure you of His faithfulness in future times of suffering?
2. Whose help do you run to first when you encounter suffering? Friends? Family? Spouse?
3. How might you take the Ebenezer of God's faithfulness up until this point in your life and raise it to Him every day?

Prayer

Pray a prayer of thanksgiving for God's repeated faithfulness in your life, asking Him for help to pursue Him instead of earthly comforts.

9. O Worship the King

———— ❖ ————

Words: Robert Grant, 1779–1838
Music: Attr. Johann Michael Hayden, 1737–1806, in *William Gardiner's Sacred Melodies*, 1815

O worship the King, all glorious above, And gratefully sing, His wonderful love; Our Shield and Defender, the Ancient of Days, Pavilioned in splendor, and girded with praise.

O tell of His might, O sing of His grace, Whose robe is the light, whose canopy space! His chariots of wrath the deep thunderclouds form, And dark is His path on the wings of the storm.

Thy bountiful care what tongue can recite? It breathes in the air, it shines in the light, It streams from the hills, it descends to the plain, And sweetly distills in the dew and the rain.

Frail children of dust, and feeble as frail, In Thee do we trust, nor find Thee to fail: Thy mercies how tender, how firm to the end, Our Maker, Defender, Redeemer, and Friend.

Bible Study Questions

1. Search the Scriptures for evidence of God being our Maker, Defender, Redeemer, and Friend.
2. What does it say about God that He expresses Himself in so many different ways?

Personal Reflection Questions

1. Rewrite this hymn using your own words. Don't worry about rhyming or melody. E.g., "Thy bountiful care what tongue can recite?" could be "Your exceeding attention, no one can even describe it."

Prayer

Pray the rewritten hymn you've written above, directing it toward the Father, Son, and Holy Spirit.

10. Sing Praise to God
Who Reigns Above

———— ✦✦ ————

Words: Johann J Schutz, 1640–1690; tr. Frances E. Cox,
    1812–1897
Music: *Bohemian Brethren's Kirchengesange*, 1566

Sing praise to God who reigns above, The God of all creation,
The God of pow'r, the God of love, The God of our salvation;
With healing balm my soul He fills, And ev'ry faithless mur-
mur stills: To God all praise and glory!

What God's almighty pow'r hath made His gracious mercy
keepeth, By morning glow or evening shade His watchful eye
ne'er sleepeth: Within the kingdom of His might, Lo! all is just
and all is right: To God all praise and glory!

The Lord is never far away, But, thro' all grief distressing, An
ever-present help and stay, Our peace and joy and blessing;
As with a mother's tender hand He leads His own, His chosen
band: To God all praise and glory!

Thus all my toilsome way along I sing aloud His praises, That all may hear the grateful song My voice unwearied raises; Be joyful in the Lord, my heart! Both soul and body bear your part: To God all praise and glory!

Bible Study Questions

1. Read Psalm 121.
2. Align parts of this hymn with parts of this psalm.

Personal Reflection Questions

1. Where does it feel as though God is slumbering or sleeping your life?
2. What would God "being awake" seem like to you?
3. What has God promised in His Word regarding His presence?

Prayer

Pray a prayer of confession for doubting the Father's goodness and faithfulness to you. Speak the truth about God from Psalm 121, applying it to your circumstances.

11. He Is Able to Deliver Thee

———— ❧ ————

Words: William A. Ogden, 1841–1897
Music: William A. Ogden, 1841–1897

'Tis the grandest theme thro' the ages rung; 'Tis the grandest theme for a mortal tongue; 'Tis the grandest theme that the world e'er sung: Our God is able to deliver thee. He is able to deliver thee, He is able to deliver thee; Tho' by sin opprest, Go to Him for rest; Our God is able to deliver thee.

'Tis the grandest theme in the earth or main; 'Tis the grandest theme for a mortal strain; 'Tis the grandest theme, tell the world again: Our God is able to deliver thee. He is able to deliver thee, He is able to deliver thee; Tho' by sin opprest, Go to Him for rest; Our God is able to deliver thee.

'Tis the grandest theme, let the tidings roll To the guilty heart, to the sinful soul; Look to God in faith, He will make thee whole: Our God is able to deliver thee. He is able to deliver

*thee, He is able to deliver thee; Tho' by sin opprest, Go to Him
for rest; Our God is able to deliver thee.*

Bible Study Questions

1. Read Daniel 3.
2. Think of a time in Scripture when God could have delivered one of His own and did not. What does it say about God that sometimes He delivers and sometimes He seems not to?

Personal Reflection Questions

1. What do you want deliverance from today?
2. Has God promised to deliver you from it here on earth?
3. What is the promise to those who are in Christ Jesus and how does it comfort you today in your specific circumstance?

Prayer

Pray a prayer of supplication to the Father. Ask Him again to deliver you, confess that you believe He can, but confess, too, that if He does not, you will trust Him still.

12. Praise the Lord Who Reigns Above

———— ✣ ————

Words: Charles Wesley, 1707–1788
Music: *Foundry Collection*, 1742

Praise the Lord who reigns above, And keeps His court below;
Praise the holy God of love, And all His greatness show; Praise
Him for His noble deeds, Praise Him for His matchless pow'r;
Him from whom all good proceeds Let earth and heav'n adore.

Celebrate th' eternal God With harp and psaltery Timbrels
soft and cymbals loud In His high praise agree; Praise Him
ev'ry tuneful string; All the reach of heav'nly art, All the
pow'rs of music bring, The music of the heart.

Him, in whom they move and live, Let ev'ry creature sing,
Glory to their Maker give, And homage to their King.
Hallowed be Hid name beneath, As in heav'n on earth adored;
Praise the Lord in ev'ry breath, Let all things praise the Lord.

Bible Study Questions

1. Read Psalm 150.
2. Why does God want to be praised?
3. Why is God worthy of praise?

Personal Reflection Questions

1. Is it easy or difficult for you to praise God with expressiveness?
2. What is a way you can express praise to God by using one of the methods in the hymn or by using another skill you have?

Prayer

Pray a prayer of adoration and worship to the Father, for all He is, all He has done, and all He will do for His name's sake.

13. Rejoice, Ye Pure in Heart

———— ❧ ————

Words: Edward H. Plumptre, 1821–1891
Music Arthur H. Messiter, 1834–1916

Rejoice, ye pure in heart, Rejoice give thanks and sing Beneath the standard of your God, The cross of Christ your King. Rejoice, rejoice, Rejoice, give thanks and sing.

Bright youth and snow-crowned age, Strong men and maidens fair, Raise high your free, exulting song, God's wondrous praise declare. Rejoice, rejoice, Rejoice, give thanks and sing.

Yes, on thro' life's long path, Still singing as ye go; From youth to age, by night and day, In gladness and in woe. Rejoice, rejoice, Rejoice, give thanks and sing.

Still lift your standard high, Still march in firm array, As warriors thro' the darkness toil Till dawns the golden day. Rejoice, rejoice, Rejoice, give thanks and sing.

Bible Study Questions

1. Read Ecclesiastes 11–12.
2. What is the way of the young in this passage?
3. What happens to the old?
4. What is the end of it all?

Personal Reflection Questions

1. Are you young, old, or somewhere in the middle?
2. In what ways do you feel more seasoned now than you did at other points in your life?
3. How has living more of your life taught you about both being young and growing old?

Prayer

Pray a prayer of confession where you admit your frailty, humanity, and need for the simplicity of the gospel in every crack and crevice of your life and heart.

14. This Is My Father's World

———— ❖ ————

Words: Maltbie D. Babcock, 1858–1901
Music: Franklin L. Sheppard, 1852–1930

This is my Father's world, and to my list'ning ears, All nature sings, and round me rings The music of the spheres. This is my Father's world, I rest me in the thought Of rocks and trees, of skies and seas; His hand the wonders wrought.

This is my Father's world, The birds their carols raise; The morning light, the lily white Declare their Maker's praise. This is my Father's world, He shines in all that's fair, In the rustling grass I hear Him pass, He speaks to me ev'rywhere.

This is my Father's world, O let me ne'er forget That though the wrong seems oft so strong, God is the Ruler yet. This is my Father's world, The battle is not done; Jesus who died shall be satisfied, And earth and heaven be one.

Bible Study Questions

1. Read Genesis 1–3.
2. In what ways was the purity of creation broken after Genesis 3?
3. How were the relationships between the earth and God, and man and God changed?

Personal Reflection Questions

1. Think of a time when you were in nature and felt deeply connected to God as the Creator of everything. How long did that feeling last? What broke it?
2. Are you ever tempted to worship the creation over the Creator? In what ways?

Prayer

Pray a prayer of confession to the Father for worshipping the creation over the Creator. Be specific in the ways you have done this.

15. For the Beauty of the Earth

———— ✤✤ ————

Words: Folliott S. Pierpoint, 1835–1917
Music: Conrad Kocher, 1786–1872; adapt. William Henry Monk,
     1823–1889

For the beauty of the earth, For the glory of the skies, For the love which from our birth Over and around us lies: Lord of all, to Thee we raise This our hymn of grateful praise.

For the wonder of each hour Of the day and of the night, Hill and wale, and tree and flow'r, Sun and moon, and stars of light: Lord of all, to Thee we raise This our hymn of grateful praise.

For the joy of human love, Brother, sister, parent, child, Friends on earth, and friends above, For all gentle thoughts and mild: Lord of all, to Thee we raise This our hymn of grateful praise.

For the church that evermore Lifteth holy hands above, Off'ring up on ev'ry shore Her pure sacrifice of love: Lord of all, to Thee we raise This our hymn of grateful praise.

For the joy of ear and ye, For the heart and mind's delight, For the mystic harmony Linking sense to sound and sight: Lord of all, to Thee we raise This our hymn of grateful praise.

For Thyself, best Gift Divine! To our race so freely giv'n; For that great, great love of Thine, Peace on earth, and joy in heav'n: Lord of all, to Thee we raise This our hymn of grateful praise.

Bible Study Questions

1. Read Galatians 2.
2. What do these verses say is the gift of God to the believer?
3. How is this gift better than any other gift? Be specific.

Personal Reflection Questions

1. When you recount your blessings, are you quicker to thank God for things than you are for the life and death of Jesus Christ? If so, why?
2. Is it a sin to be thankful for the created things?
3. How can you keep any created thing from becoming an idol?

Prayer

Pray a prayer of confession for the ways you have worshipped the creation over the Creator. Ask the Holy Spirit to help you rightly order your worship.

16. All Things Bright and Beautiful

———— ✤ ————

Words: Cecil F. Alexander, 1818–1895
Music: 17th Century, adapt. from Louis Spohr, 1784–1859

All things bright and beautiful, All things great and small, All things wide and wonderful; Our Father made them all. Each little flower that opens, Each little bird that sings; He made their glowing colors, He made their tiny wings.

Cold wind in the winter, Pleasant summer sun, Ripe fruits in the garden; He made them ev'ry one. He gave us eyes to see them, And lips that we might tell How good is God our Father Who doeth all things well.

Bible Study Questions

1. Read Genesis 1.
2. What word does God use to describe creation?

3. Why do you think God didn't use a word like *beautiful* or *perfect*?

Personal Reflection Questions

1. Think of some natural occurrences in nature that are not pleasant or beautiful. Are these occurrences still *good*?
2. Think about your own life. What in it is painful or confusing?
3. How might God call these experiences good?

Prayer

Pray a prayer of supplication. Ask the Father to give you supernatural insight into your life and the lives of others, to see where He is rightly ordering things for your good and His glory.

17. Guide Me, O Thou Great Jehovah

————— ❧ —————

Words: William Williams, 1717–1791
Music: John Hughes, 1873–1932

Guide me, O Thou great Jehovah, Pilgrim through this barren land; I am weak, but Thou art mighty; Hold me with Thy pow'rful hand; Bread of heaven, Bread of heaven, Feed me till I want no more, Feed me till I want no more.

Open now the crystal fountain, Whence the healing stream doth flow; Let the fire and cloudy pillar Lead me all my journey through; Strong Deliverer, strong Deliverer, Be Thou still my strength and shield, Be Thou still my strength and shield.

When I tread the verge of Jordan, Bid my anxious fears subside; Bear me thro' the swelling current, Land me safe on Canaan's side; Songs of praises, songs of praises I will ever give to Thee, I will ever give to Thee.

Bible Study Questions

1. Read Joshua 3.
2. Think of another time God led the Israelites through a body of water on dry ground. Was that body of water bigger or smaller than the Jordan River?
3. Do you think the Israelites were more or less afraid this time?

Personal Reflection Questions

1. Think of a time God carried you through a period of confusion or suffering. In what ways was His character displayed to you and which attributes stand out most in your heart from that period?
2. Think of a situation in front of you that seems scary or unknown. How does remembering God's character from your past encourage and strengthen you to walk through this?

Prayer

Pray a prayer of thanksgiving for God's faithfulness not only to you but to His name. Read Isaiah 42:1 and ask the Holy Spirit for comfort as He walks through the next season with you.

18. If You Will Only Let God Guide You

———— ❧ ————

Words: Georg Beunark, 1621–1681
Music: Georg Beunark, 1621–1681

If you will only let God guide you, And hope in Him thro' all your ways, Whatever comes, He'll stand beside you, To bear you thro' the evil days; Who trusts in God's unchanging love Builds on the Rock that cannot move.

Only be still, and wait His leisure In cheerful hope, with heart content To take whate'er the Father's pleasure And all discerning love have sent; Nor doubt our inmost wants are known To Him who chose us for His own.

Sing, pray, and swerve not from His ways, But do your part in conscience true; Trust His rich promises of grace, So shall they be fulfilled in you; God hears the call of those in need, The souls that trust in Him indeed.

Bible Study Questions

1. Read Exodus 14.
2. Were the Israelites trusting or doubting?
3. Why do you think the words of Moses were firm, "Fear ye not, stand still. . . . The LORD shall fight for you, and ye shall hold your peace" (v. 13–14), instead of gentle and coddling?

Personal Reflection Questions

1. When you are afraid, do you respond better to firm truth or watered-down words? Which bolsters your faith?
2. When others around you are afraid, do you give them watered-down words or truth from Scripture?

Prayer

Pray a prayer of repentance for not always speaking the truth in love to yourself and others. Ask the Holy Spirit for help as you endeavor to speak the truth with cheerful hope and a content heart.

19. Like a River Glorious

———— ❧ ————

Words: Frances R. Havergal, 1836–1879
Music: James Mountain, 1844–1933

Like a river glorious Is God's perfect peace, Over all victorious In its bright increase; Perfect, yet it floweth Fuller ev'ry day; Perfect, yet it growth Deeper all the way. Stayed upon Jehovah, Hearts are fully blessed; Finding, as He promised, Perfect peace and rest.

Hidden in the hollow Of His blessed hand, Never foe can follow, Never traitor stand; Not a surge of worry, Not a shade of care, Not a blast of hurry Touch the spirit there. Stayed upon Jehovah, Hearts are fully blessed; Finding, as He promised, Perfect peace and rest.

Ev'ry joy or trial Falleth from above, Trac'd upon our dial By the Sun of Love; We may trust Him fully All for us to do; They who trust Him wholly Find Him wholly true. Stayed upon Jehovah, Hearts are fully blessed; Finding, as He promised, Perfect peace and rest.

Bible Study Questions

1. Read Isaiah 26.
2. Does this passage only speak of the peaceful aspects of a life with God?
3. Why does Isaiah warn the people there is danger ahead?

Personal Reflection Questions

1. Do you believe God ordains "ev'ry joy or trial," that they all "falleth from above"?
2. What does it say about God that sometimes He allows us to go through trials?
3. Do you find it easy or difficult to keep your mind stayed on Him during trials?
4. What might God be trying to show you through your trials?

Prayer

Pray a prayer of thanksgiving to the Father, thanking Him for keeping you and giving you the perfect peace and assurance of His love by sending His Son to die on the cross and rise again to bring you newness of life in the midst of trials and sufferings.

20. Abide with Me

———— ✤ ————

Words: Henry F. Lyte, 1793–1847
Music: William Henry Monk, 1823–1889

Abide with me: fast falls the eventide; The darkness deepend;
Lord, with me abide: When other helpers fail, and comforts
flee, Help of the helpless, O abide with me!

Swift to its close ebbs out life's little day; Earth's joys grow
dim, its glories pass away; Change and decay in guide and
stay can be? Thro' cloud and sunshine, O abide with me!

I need Thy presence ev'ry passing hour; What but Thy grace
can foil the tempter's pow'r? Who like Thyself my guide and
say can be? Thro' cloud and sunshine, O abide with me!

Hold Thou Thy cross before my closing eyes; Shine thro' the
gloom, and point me to the skies: Heav'n's morning breaks
and earth's vain shadows flee: In life, in death, O Lord, abide
with me!

Bible Study Questions

1. Read John 14–16.
2. How does Jesus talk about abiding? Make a list of all the times He mentioned the word *abide*. Who did the abiding in each occurrence? What were they abiding in?
3. Does Jesus abide in us more or we in Him in this passage?
4. Who does Jesus say He is sending to abide in us in chapter 16?

Personal Reflection Questions

1. How does knowing the Holy Spirit abides in you change how you trust the care of the Father and the work of the Son?
2. Where is an area in your life today where you need to trust the Holy Spirit to help, comfort, and teach you?
3. What would depending on the Holy Spirit mean for you today?

Prayer

Pray a prayer of repentance for abiding in your own strength more than you trust the Holy Spirit and abide in the strength He gives. Ask the Holy Spirit to increase your trust and to make you more aware of His abiding presence.

21. God Will Take Care of You

———— ❖ ————

Words: Civilla D. Martin, 1869–1948
Music: W. Stillman Martin, 1862–1935

Be not dismayed whate'er betide, God will take care of you;
Beneath His wings of love abide, God will take care of you.
God will take care of you, Through ev'ry day, o'er all the way;
He will take care of you, God will take care of you.

Thro' days of toil when heart doth fail, God will take care of
you; When dangers fierce your path assail, God will take care
of you. God will take care of you, Through ev'ry day, o'er all
the way; He will take care of you, God will take care of you.

No matter what may be the test, God will take care of you;
Lean, weary one, upon His breast, God will take care of you.
God will take care of you, Through ev'ry day, o'er all the way;
He will take care of you, God will take care of you.

Bible Study Questions

1. Read Luke 12:22–34.
2. Why do you think Jesus used the example of birds, flowers, and grass instead of other humans?
3. Think of someone in Scripture whom God cared for or fed in a miraculous way. Were they anxious? What did God say to their anxiety?

Personal Reflection Questions

1. What are you anxious about today?
2. If you were to lose the thing you fear losing (control, your job, a relationship, etc.) what would happen?
3. Would God still be on His throne and caring for you without that thing?

Prayer

Pray of a prayer of confession for not trusting the God who promises to care for you. Ask the Lord for more trust in the words of Scripture and the truth within it, and ask that the Holy Spirit would comfort you in your anxiety.

22. Grace Greater Than Our Sin

———— ❧ ————

Words: Julia H. Johnston, 1849–1919
Music: Daniel B. Towner, 1850–1919

Marvelous grace of our loving Lord, Grace that exceeds our sin and our guilt, Yonder on Calvary's mount outpoured, There where the blood of the Lamb was spilt. Grace, grace, God's grace, Grace that will pardon and cleanse with-in; Grace, grace, God's grace, Grace that is greater than all our sin.

Dark is the stain that we cannot hide, What can avail to wash it away? Look! there is flowing a crimson tide; Whiter than snow you may be today. Grace, grace, God's grace, Grace that will pardon and cleanse with-in; Grace, grace, God's grace, Grace that is greater than all our sin.

Marvelous, infinite, matchless grace, Freely bestowed on all who believe; All who are longing to see His face, Will you this moment His grace receive? Grace, grace, God's grace, Grace that will pardon and cleanse with-in; Grace, grace, God's grace, Grace that is greater than all our sin.

Bible Study Questions

1. Read Ephesians 3:14–21.
2. What precludes having the strength to comprehend the love of God?

Personal Reflection Questions

1. How many are your sins?
2. How great is God's love for you?
3. Do you believe God's grace really is greater than all your sins? Why or why not? Do you live like it?

Prayer

Pray a prayer of worship and adoration, thanking God for His grace, for the blood of Christ that covers your sin, and for the greatness of God's love.

23. Love Lifted Me

Words: James Rowe, 1865–1933
Music: Howard E. Smith, 1863–1918

I was sinking deep in sin, far from the peaceful shore, Very deeply stained within, sinking to rise no more; But the Master f the sea heard my despairing cry, From the waters lifted me now safe am I. Love lifted me! Love lifted me! When nothing else could help, Love lifted me.

All my heart to Him I give, ever to Him I'll cling, In His blessed presence live, ever His praises sing; Love so mighty and so true merits my soul's best songs; Faithful loving service, too, to Him belongs. Love lifted me! Love lifted me! When nothing else could help, Love lifted me.

Souls in danger, look above, Jesus completely saves; He will lift you by His love out of the angry waves; He's the Master of the sea, billows His will obey; He your Savior wants to be, be saved today. Love lifted me! Love lifted me! When nothing else could help, Love lifted me.

Bible Study Questions

1. Read Matthew 14:22–33.
2. How did Peter's fear relate to him sinking?
3. What does this passage say about the character of man? About the character of Jesus?

Personal Reflection Questions

1. Think of a time when you were sure God was calling you to do something. Did you ever feel afraid in that process?
2. What was the result when you began to fear?
3. What are you fearing today?
4. What does God's Word say to your fear?

Prayer

Pray a prayer of confession and repentance for any doubts you have about God's ability to carry you through until the end. Ask Him for the gift of faith, not to stay afloat, but to keep your eyes on Him.

24. O Love That Will Not Let Me Go

———— ✥ ————

Words: George Matheson, 1842–1906
Music: Albert L. Peace, 1844–1912

*O Love that wilt not let me go, I rest my weary soul in Thee;
I give Thee back the life I owe, That in Thine ocean depths its
flow May richer, fuller be.*

*O Light that foll'west all my way, I yield my flick'ring torch
to Thee; My heart restores its borrowed ray, That in Thy sunshine's glow its day May brighter, fairer be.*

*O Joy that sleekest me thro' pain, I cannot close my heart to
Thee; I trace the rainbow thro' the rain, And feel the promise
is not vain That morn shall tearless be.*

*O Cross that liftest up my head, I dare not ask to hide from
Thee; I lay in dust life's glory dead, And from the ground there
blossoms red, Life that shall endless be.*

Bible Study Questions

1. Read Psalm 36.
2. Make a list of what God gives to those He loves.
3. Make a list of what the children of God do or have.

Personal Reflection Questions

1. Which comes more naturally to you: to feel or to know the love of God?
2. Why do you think you struggle with whichever one is less natural for you?
3. What do this passage and the hymn say to that less natural inclination toward the love of God?

Prayer

Pray a prayer of supplication, asking God to reveal His love to you in knowledge and to increase your love for Him in varied ways.

25. He Keeps Me Singing

———— ✢ ————

Words: Luther B. Bridgers, 1884-1948
Music: Luther B. Bridgers, 1884–1948

There's within my heart a melody; Jesus whispers sweet and low, "Fear not, I am with thee, peace, be still," In all of life's ebb and flow. Jesus, Jesus, Jesus, Sweetest name I know, Fills my ev'ry longing, Keeps me singing as I go.

All my life was wrecked by sin and strife, Discord filled my heart with pain, Jesus swept across the broken strings, Stirred the slumb'ring chords again. Jesus, Jesus, Jesus, Sweetest name I know, Fills my ev'ry longing, Keeps me singing as I go.

Feasting on the riches of His grace, Resting 'neath His heart with pain, Jesus swept across the broken strings, Stirred the slumb'ring chords again. Jesus, Jesus, Jesus, Sweetest name I know, Fills my ev'ry longing, Keeps me singing as I go.

Tho' sometimes He leads thro' waters deep, Trials fall across the way; Thro' sometimes the path seems rough and steep, See His footprints all the way. Jesus, Jesus, Jesus, Sweetest name I know, Fills my ev'ry longing, Keeps me singing as I go.

Soon He's coming back to welcome me Far beyond the starry sky; I shall wing my flight to worlds unknown, I shall reign with Him on high. Jesus, Jesus, Jesus, Sweetest name I know, Fills my ev'ry longing, Keeps me singing as I go.

Bible Study Questions

1. Read Matthew 4:1–11.
2. Who led Jesus into the wilderness where He was tempted?
3. Who came and ministered to Jesus at the conclusion of His time in the wilderness?

Personal Reflection Questions

1. Think of a time when you were "wrecked with sin and strife, discord filling your life with pain." Where do you see the presence of God in that time?
2. How do you see the presence of God today in the midst of difficult things?
3. What fills your mouth when you face temptation?

Prayer

Pray a prayer of thanksgiving for being kept by God in every season and circumstance of your life. Worship Jesus for being the "sweetest name you know" in the midst of those circumstances.

26. Praise Him! Praise Him!

——— ✤ ———

Words: Fanny J. Crosby, 1820–1915
Music: Chester G. Allen, 1838–1878

Praise Him! praise Him! Jesus, our blessed Redeemer! Sing O earth, His wonderful love proclaim! Hail Him! hail Him! highest archangels in glory, Strength and honor give to His holy name! Like a shepherd, Jesus will guard His children; In His arms He carries them all day long: Praise Him! praise Him! tell of His excellent greatness! Praise Him! praise Him! ever in joyful song!

Praise Him! praise Him! Jesus, our blessed Redeemer! For our sins, He suffered and bled and died; He our Rock, our hope of eternal salvation, Hail Him! hail Him! Jesus the crucified: Sound His praises! Jesus who bore our sorrows, Love unbounded, wonderful, deep, and strong: Praise Him! praise Him! tell of His excellent greatness! Praise Him! praise Him! ever in joyful song!

Praise Him! praise Him! Jesus, our blessed Redeemer! Heav'nly portals loud with hosannas ring! Jesus, Savior, reigneth forever and ever; Crown Him! crown Him! prophet and priest and King! Christ is coming, over the world victorious, Pow'r and glory unto the Lord belong: Praise Him! praise Him! tell of His excellent greatness! Praise Him! praise Him! ever in joyful song!

Bible Study Questions

1. Search the Scriptures to find an instance of Jesus being a prophet, priest, or king.
2. How does Jesus fulfill the role of prophet, priest, or king in the passage you found?
3. How might the original hearers have understood this passage?

Personal Reflection Questions

1. How do you most naturally see the role of Jesus in your life and the lives of others? As prophet? As priest? As king?
2. What role do you struggle to see Him fulfilling? Why?

3. What is one thing you could do today to remember Jesus is perfectly fulfilling all of these roles in the world today?

Prayer

Pray a prayer of adoration for the ways in which God has made Himself known to you as Father, Son, and Holy Spirit, as Prophet, Priest, and King. Ask the Father to give you the gift of faith to increase your knowledge of Him in all ways.

27. This Is the Day the Lord Has Made

———— ✤ ————

Words: Isaac Watts, 1674–1748,
Music: Thomas A Arne, 1710–1778

*This is the day the Lord has made; He calls the hours His own;
Let heav'n rejoice, let earth be glad, And praise surround the
throne.*

*Today He rose and left the dead, And Satan's empire fell;
Today the saints His triumph spread, And all His wonders tell.*

*Hosanna to th'anointed King, To David's holy Son: Help us, O
Lord! descend and bring Salvation from Your throne.*

*Blest be the Lord, who comes to us With messages of grace;
Who comes, in God His Father's name, To save our sinful race.*

Bible Study Questions

1. Read Psalm 118.
2. Make a list of all the things man *does* and *is* in this passage.
3. Make a list of all the things the Lord *does* and *is*.

Personal Reflection Questions

1. How do you view the present? Are you waiting for the phase you are in to finish so you can get to the "good stuff"?
2. How does viewing today as a gift from God change how you view your portion today?
3. Has God promised you tomorrow?

Prayer

Pray a prayer of repentance and confession to the Father. Ask Him to give you faith enough to see this day through, to trust Him to care for all your tomorrows.

28. Were You There?

———— ✛ ————

Words: Negro Spiritual
Music: Adapt. John W. Work Jr., 1872–1925 and Fredrick J.
  Work, 1879–1942

*Were you there when they crucified my Lord? Were you there
when the crucified my Lord? Oh! Sometimes it causes me to
tremble, tremble, tremble. Were you there when they crucified my Lord?*

*Were you there when they nailed Him to the tree? Were you
there when they nailed Him to the tree? Oh! Sometimes it
causes me to tremble, tremble, tremble. Were you there when
they nailed Him to the tree?*

*Were you there when they laid Him in the tomb? Were you
there when they laid Him in the tomb? Oh! Sometimes it
causes me to tremble, tremble, tremble. Were you there when
they laid Him in the tomb?*

Were you there when He rose up from the grave? Were you there when He rose up from the grave? Oh! Sometimes it causes me to tremble, tremble, tremble. Were you there when He rose up from the grave?

Bible Study Questions

1. Read Matthew 27:32–56.
2. What do you think those witnessing the crucifixion thought about who Jesus was at that point?
3. Search the Scriptures to find the prophecies that described all that would happen.

Personal Reflection Questions

1. Has there been a time when something bad happened that you were sure wouldn't?
2. Did you feel let down by God or man in that moment?
3. Looking back now, can see you how God never failed you or failed to keep His promises from Scripture?

Prayer

Pray a prayer of worship to the Father for always keeping His promises, for never failing to stay true to His Word. Worship Him for His unchangeableness.

29. Christ the Lord Is Risen Today

———— ✿ ————

Words: Charles Wesley, 1707–1788
Music: Lyra Davidica, 1708

Christ the Lord is ris'n today Alleluia! Sons of men and angels say, Alleluia! Raise your joys and triumphs high, Alleluia! Sing, ye heav'ns, and earth, reply, Alleluia!

Lives again our glorious King, Alleluia! Where, O Death, is now thy sting? Alleluia! Dying once He all doth save, Alleluia! Where thy victory, O Grave? Alleluia!

Love's redeeming work is done, Alleluia! Fought the fight, the battle won, Alleluia! Death in vain forbids Him rise, Alleluia! Christ hath opened Paradise, Alleluia!

Soar we now where Christ has led, Alleluia! Foll'wing our exalted Head, Alleluia! Made like Him, like Him we rise, Alleluia! Ours the cross, the grave, the skies, Alleluia!

Bible Study Questions

1. Read Matthew 28.
2. Why were the men and women told to not be afraid?
3. Do you think they grasped the fullness of what was occurring?

Personal Reflection Questions

1. Is it easy or hard for you to believe in the resurrection? Why or why not?
2. Why was the resurrection necessary?
3. Do you always feel the work of redemption is done? Why or why not?

Prayer

Pray a prayer of supplication, asking the Father to increase your faith and enlarge your capacity for the supernatural work for the Spirit.

30. Low in the Grave He Lay

———— ✤ ————

Words: Robert Lowry, 1826–1899
Music: Robert Lowry, 1826–1899

Low in the grave He lay, Jesus, my Savior! Waiting the coming day, Jesus, my Lord! Up from the grave He arose, With a mighty triumph o'er His foes; He arose a victor from the dark domain, And He lives forever with His saints to reign. He arose! He arose! Hallelujah! Christ rose!

Vainly they watch His bed, Jesus, my Savior! Vainly they seal the dead, Jesus, my Lord! Up from the grave He arose, With a mighty triumph o'er His foes; He arose a victor from the dark domain, And He lives forever with His saints to reign. He arose! He arose! Hallelujah! Christ rose!

Death cannot keep his prey, Jesus, my Savior! He tore the bars away, Jesus, my Lord! Up from the grave He arose, With a mighty triumph o'er His foes; He arose a victor from the dark domain, And He lives forever with His saints to reign. He arose! He arose! Hallelujah! Christ rose!

Bible Study Questions

1. Read Psalm 49:15 in multiple translations.
2. What is meant by Sheol or "the grave"?
3. Why did Jesus have to go there?

Personal Reflection Questions

1. When you consider your sin, where do you envision it being: in Sheol, nailed to the cross, on you, etc.?
2. If you are a child of God, where is your sin forevermore?
3. Which sins do you struggle to believe Christ has paid for?

Prayer

Pray a prayer of worship to Jesus for paying for your sins (past, present, future), for dealing with them completely (removing them as far as the east is from the west). Ask the Spirit to help you live and walk as though you believe that completely.

31. Crown Him with Many Crowns

———— ✤ ————

Words: St. 1, 3, 4, Matthew Bridges, 1800–1894; st. 2, Godfrey
        Thring, 1823–1903
Music: George J. Elvey, 1816–1893

*Crown Him with many crowns, The Lamb upon His throne;
Hark! how the heav'nly anthem drowns All music but its own:
Awake, my soul, and sing Of Him who died for thee, And hail
Him as thy matchless King Thro' all eternity.*

*Crown Him the Lord of life, Who triumphed o'er the grave,
And rose victorious in the strife For those He came to save;
His glories now we sing Who died, and rose on high, Who
died eternal life to bring, And lives that death may die.*

*Crown Him the Lord of peace, Whose pow'r a scepter sways
From pole to pole, that wars may cease, And all by pray'r and
praise: All hail, Redeemer, hail! For Thou hast died for me:
Fair flow'rs of paradise extend Their fragrance ever sweet.*

Crown Him the Lord of love; Behold His hands and side, Those wounds, yet visible above, In beauty glorified: All hail, Redeemer, hail! For Thou hast died for me: Thy praise and glory shall not fail Thro'out eternity.

Bible Study Questions

1. Read Hebrews 2:5–18.
2. Who in this passage is wearing crowns?
3. For what reason, does the Scripture say, are they each wearing crowns?

Personal Reflection Questions

1. Do you pursue righteousness in your life because you desire a crown or because Jesus is King?
2. How are those different motivations and what would the long-term pursuit of each result in?

Prayer

Pray a prayer of supplication to the Father, asking Him to help you see Jesus as King of your life and not you as ruler over your life. Praise and worship Jesus for doing everything necessary to wear the crown righteously.

32. We Welcome Glad Easter

---- ❀ ----

Words: Anonymous
Music: Welsh Hymn Tune

We welcome glad Easter when Jesus arose, And won a great victory over His foes. Then raise your glad voices, all Christians, and sing, Bring glad Easter praises to Jesus, your King.

We tell how the women came early that day, And there at the tomb found the stone rolled away. Then raise your glad voices, all Christians, and sing, Bring glad Easter praises to Jesus, your King.

We sing of the angel who said: "Do not fear! Your Savior is risen, and He is not here." Then raise your glad voices, all Christians, and sing, Bring glad Easter praises to Jesus, your King.

We think of the promise which Jesus did give: "That he who believes in Me also shall live!" Then raise your glad voices, all Christians, and sing, Bring glad Easter praises to Jesus, your King.

Bible Study Questions

1. Read John 11.
2. Why do you think John put the narrative of Lazarus right before the plot to kill Jesus? What was he trying to show the readers?

Personal Reflection Questions

1. Do you feel alive today? Why or why not?
2. What things, circumstances, beliefs, or sins are pressing you closer to the grave than to life in Christ?
3. What would you lose if you were to give up this thing, circumstance, belief, or sin?

Prayer

Pray a prayer of confession to the Father, asking Him for help to believe—really believe, deep in your heart—the words of Christ: that He who believes in Him shall live.

33. Look, Ye Saints! The Sight Is Glorious

———— ✤ ————

Words: Thomas Kelly, 1769–1855
Music: William Owen, 1814–1893

Look, ye saints! the sight is glorious: See the Man of Sorrows now; From the fight returned victorious, Ev'ry knee to Him shall bow; Crown Him, crown Him, Crown Him, crown Him, Crown Him, crown Him. Crowns become the Victor's brow, Crowns become the Victor's brow.

Crown the Savior! angels, crown Him; Rich the trophies Jesus brings; In the seat of pow'r enthrone Him, While the vault of heaven rings: Crown Him, crown Him, Crown Him, crown Him, Crown Him, crown Him. Crown the Savior King of kings, Crown the Savior King of kings.

Sinners in derision crowned Him, Mocking thus the Savior's claim; Saints and angels crowd around Him, Own His title, praise His name. Crown Him, crown Him, Crown Him, crown Him, Crown Him, crown Him. Spread abroad the Victor's fame, Spread abroad the Victor's fame.

Hark, those bursts of acclamation! Hark, those loud triumphant chords! Jesus takes the highest station; O what joy the sight affords! Crown Him, crown Him, Crown Him, crown Him, Crown Him, crown Him. King of kings, and Lord of lords! King of kings, and Lord of lords!

Bible Study Questions

1. Read Matthew 27:29.
2. What does this scene point toward (Philippians 2:1–11)?
3. Who will acknowledge Jesus as King one day?

Personal Reflection Questions

1. Think of someone who seems beyond the redemption of Christ: a neighbor, a family member, a terrorist, a murderer.
2. Think of someone in Scripture who was those things and whom God chose to save.

3. With that second person in mind, pray and ask the Father to save, redeem, and set free the first person.

Prayer

Pray a prayer of confession and repentance for believing, however minutely, that this individual was beyond the grace and forgiveness of Christ. If you need to forgive them, ask for the Spirit's help.

34. "Man of Sorrows," What a Name

———— ❧ ————

Words: Philip P. Bliss, 1838–1876
Music: Philip P. Bliss, 1838–1876

*"Man of sorrows!" what a name For the Son of God who came
Ruined sinners to reclaim! Hallelujah, what a Savior!*

*Bearing shame and scoffing rude, In my place condemned He
stood, Seal'd my pardon with His blood; Hallelujah, what a
Savior!*

*Guilty, vile, and helpless we, Spotless Lamb of God was He;
Full atonement! can it be? Hallelujah, what a Savior!*

*Lifted up was He to die, "It is finished," was His cry; Now in
heav'n exalted high, Hallelujah, what a Savior!*

*When He comes, our glorious King, All His ransomed home
in bring, Then anew this song we'll sing, Hallelujah, what a
Savior!*

Bible Study Questions

1. Read Isaiah 53.
2. Make a list of all the things "he" is from this passage.
3. Find evidence of Jesus in the gospels fulfilling these words from Isaiah.

Personal Reflection Questions

1. Using the list above, have you ever felt any of those things yourself?
2. How does seeing how Jesus embodied those things in the New Testament help you see your circumstances differently?
3. Which of these characteristics or circumstances of Jesus remind you today of how loved you are by Him?

Prayer

Pray a prayer of worship to Jesus for becoming sin so that you didn't have to. Praise Him for bearing all the sorrow and grief and pain so you didn't have to. Ask the Spirit for help in living as though those things were true.

35. What a Friend We Have in Jesus

———— ✤✤ ————

Words: Joseph Scriven, 1819–1886
Music: Charles C. Converse, 1832-1918

What a friend we have in Jesus, All our sins and griefs to bear!
What a privilege to carry Ev'rything to God in prayer! Oh,
what peace we often forfeit, Oh what needless pain we bear,
All because we do not carry Ev'rything to God in prayer!

Have we trials and temptations? Is there trouble anywhere?
We should never be discouraged, Take it to the Lord in prayer:
Can we find a friend so faithful Who will all our sorrows
share? Jesus knows our ev'ry weakness, Take it to the Lord
in prayer.

Are we weak and heavy laden, Cumbered with a load of care?
Precious Savior, still our refuge; Take it to the Lord in prayer:
Do thy friends despise, forsake thee? Take it to the Lord in
prayer; In His arms He'll take and shield thee; Thou wilt find
a solace there.

Bible Study Questions

1. Read Luke 7.
2. Jesus reprimanded the people for saying John the Baptist had a demon because he did not eat bread or drink wine and for calling Jesus a drunkard and glutton for doing the opposite. What was He trying to communicate to them?

Personal Reflection Questions

1. Think of a time when you felt there was no course of action ahead of you that wouldn't be critiqued by others. How does this passage help you?
2. Are we to be faithful to an outcome or to the Word of God?
3. What does the Word of God say to your situation?

Prayer

Pray a prayer of thanksgiving to Jesus, for showing us the inability we have to please everyone at all times. Thank Him for being a friend to sinners and ask Him for help for you to do the same.

36. Jesus Is All the World to Me

———— ✦ ————

Words: Will I. Thompson, 1847–1909
Music: Will I. Thompson, 1847–1909

Jesus is all the world to me, My life, my joy, my all; He is my strength from day to day, Without Him I would fall: When I am sad, to Him I go; No other one can cheer me so; When I am sad, He makes me glad; He's my friend.

Jesus is all the world to me, My friend in trials sore; I go to Him for blessings, and He gives them o'er and o'er: He sends the sunshine and the rain, He sends the harvest's golden grain; Sunshine and rain, harvest of grain; He's my friend.

Jesus is all the world to me, And true to him I'll be; Oh, how could I this friend deny, When He's so true to me? Following Him, I know I'm right, He watches o'er me day and night; Following Him, by day and night; He's my friend.

Jesus is all the world to me, I want no better friend; I trust Him now, I'll trust Him when Life's fleeting days shall end: Beautiful life with such a friend, Beautiful life that has no end; Eternal life, eternal joy; He's my friend.

Bible Study Questions

1. Read Philippians 1:12–30.
2. What does Paul mean when he says "to live is Christ, and to die is gain" (v. 21)?
3. What does this passage say about those who walk with Christ?

Personal Reflection Questions

1. Do you look for earthly gain as you serve Jesus?
2. What is your measure of success in your Christian life? Why?
3. What does Scripture say to those who walk with Christ?

Prayer

Pray a prayer of repentance for the ways you have sought the gifts more than the Giver Himself. Ask the Spirit for help as you serve in unseen ways on earth.

37. In the Garden

———— ❀ ————

Words: C. Austin Miles, 1868–1946
Music: C. Austin Miles, 1868–1946

*I come to the garden alone, While the dew is still on the roses;
And the voice I hear, falling on my ear, The Son of God discloses. And He walks with me, and He talks with me, And He
tells me I am His own, And the joy we share as we tarry there,
None other has ever known.*

*He speaks, and the sound of His voice Is so sweet the birds
hush their singing; And the melody that He gave to me Within
my heart is ringing. And He walks with me, and He talks with
me, And He tells me I am His own, And the joy we share as we
tarry there, None other has ever known.*

*I'd stay in the garden with him Tho' the night around me be
falling; But He bids me go; thro' the voice of woe, His voice to
me is calling. And He walks with me, and He talks with me,*

And He tells me I am His own, And the joy we share as we tarry there, None other has ever known.

Bible Study Questions

1. Read Genesis 5:24.
2. What else is known about Enoch? Search the Scriptures for more on his life.
3. Were his life and accomplishments enough?

Personal Reflection Questions

1. Do you have a list of things you want to accomplish for Jesus or the Church or for your own life?
2. What about the life of Enoch is encouraging to you?
3. Can you say that you walk with God in the ways this hymn speaks about? Why or why not?

Prayer

Pray a prayer of worship and adoration to the Father for inviting you to walk with Him and for sending the Spirit to live within you, empowering you and helping you as you live.

38. The Great Physician

— ✣ —

Words: William Hunter, 1811–1877
Music: John H. Stockton, 1813–1877

The great Physician now is near, The sympathizing Jesus; He speaks the dropping heart to sheer, Oh! hear the voice of Jesus. Sweetest note in seraph song, Sweetest name on mortal tongue; Sweetest carol ever sung, Jesus, blessed Jesus.

Your many sins are all forgiv'n, Oh! hear the voice of Jesus; Go on your way in peace to heav'n, And wear a crown with Jesus. Sweetest note in seraph song, Sweetest name on mortal tongue; Sweetest carol ever sung, Jesus, blessed Jesus.

All glory to the dying Lamb! I now believe in Jesus; I love the blessed Savior's name, I love the name of Jesus. Sweetest note in seraph song, Sweetest name on mortal tongue; Sweetest carol ever sung, Jesus, blessed Jesus.

His name dispels my guilt and fear, No other name but Jesus;
Oh! how my soul delights to hear The charming name of
Jesus. Sweetest note in seraph song, Sweetest name on mortal
tongue; Sweetest carol ever sung, Jesus, blessed Jesus.

Bible Study Questions

1. Read John 5:1–9.
2. Was the question answered that Jesus asked in verse 6?
3. Think of another time in Scripture when God asked a person a question and they deflected by not directly answering Him. Why do you think people do that?

Personal Reflection Questions

1. Are there questions you feel God is asking of you and you do not answer? Why or why not?
2. Is God ever surprised by your answers?
3. Why do you try to hide from Him?

Prayer

Pray a prayer of thanksgiving to Jesus for coming for the sick and not the well, for helping you realize that without your sin-sickness, you have no need for Him. Praise Him for saving you.

39. One Day

———— ❧ ————

Words: J. Wilbur Chapman, 1859–1918
Music: Charles H. Marsh, 1886–1956

One day when heaven was filled with His praises, One day when sin was as black as could be, Jesus came forth to be born of a virgin, Dwelt among men, my example is He! Living, He loved me; dying, He saved me; Buried, He carried my sins far away; Rising, He justified freely forever: One day He's coming—O glorious day!

One day they led Him up Calvary's mountain, One day they nailed Him to die on the tree; Suffering anguish, despised and rejected: Bearing our sins, my Redeemer is He! Living, He loved me; dying, He saved me; Buried, He carried my sins far away; Rising, He justified freely forever: One day He's coming—O glorious day!

One day they left Him alone in the garden, One day He rested, from suffering free; Angels came down o'er His death He had conquered; Now is ascended, my Lord evermore! Living, He loved me; dying, He saved me; Buried, He carried my sins far away; Rising, He justified freely forever: One day He's coming—O glorious day!

One day the grave could conceal Him no longer, One day the stone rolled away from the door; Then He arose, over death He had conquered; Now is ascended, my Lord evermore! Living, He loved me; dying, He saved me; Buried, He carried my sins far away; Rising, He justified freely forever: One day He's coming—O glorious day!

One day the trumpet will sound for His coming, One day the skies with His glories will shine; Wonderful day, my beloved One bringing; Glorious Savior, this Jesus is mine! Living, He loved me; dying, He saved me; Buried, He carried my sins far away; Rising, He justified freely forever: One day He's coming—O glorious day!

Bible Study Questions

1. Read 1 Corinthians 15:35–58.
2. Make a list of what man does in this passage and what God (Father, Son, Holy Spirit) does.

Personal Reflection Questions

1. Think of ways you've tried to accomplish the work of Christ on your own behalf. Why have you done that?
2. What need would you have for Christ if you could accomplish all He did?
3. Does Christ need your help? Does He desire it? Why? And how could you help?

Prayer

Pray a prayer of repentance for making your part in the work of the gospel larger than it is. Praise God for completing the gospel from start to finish, and for inviting you into it.

40. Lo, He Comes with Clouds Descending

———— ✤ ————

Words: St. 1, 2, 4, Charles Wesley, 1707–1788; st. 3, John
  Cennick, 1718–1755
Music: Henry T. Smart, 1813–1879

*Lo, He comes with clouds descending, Once for favored sin-
ners slain; Thousand thousand saints attending Swell the triumph of His train: Alleluia, alleluia! God appears on earth to
reign.*

*Ev'ry eye shall now behold Him, Robed in splendor's majesty;
Those who set at naught and sold Him, Pierced and nailed
Him to the tree, Deeply wailing, deeply wailing, Shall the true
Messiah see.*

*Now the Savior, long expected, See, in solemn pomp appear;
All who have not Him rejected Now shall meet Him in the air:
Alleluia, alleluia! See the day of God appear.*

Yea, amen, let all adore Thee, High on Thine eternal throne; Savior, take the pow'r and glory, Claim the kingdom for Thine own: Oh, come quickly, oh, come quickly! Everlasting God, come down.

Bible Study Questions

1. Read Matthew 24:29–31.
2. What do you think the original hearers thought about the words of Jesus here?
3. What do you think they thought of these words after the crucifixion of Jesus?

Personal Reflection Questions

1. Do you wait eagerly for the coming of Christ? Why or why not?
2. How does your waiting, or lack of it, show in your life?
3. What would the life of a person who waits eagerly for the coming of Christ look like?

Prayer

Pray a prayer of supplication to the Father, asking for the help of the Holy Spirit to live as though Christ's return is imminent. Repent for ways you have been lazy in your walk with Christ on earth.

41. All Hail the Power of Jesus' Name

———— ✢ ————

Words: St. 1, 2, Edward Perronet, 1726–1792; st. 3, 4, John
    Rippon, 1751–1836
Music: Oliver Holden, 1765–1844

All hail the pow'r of Jesus' name! Let angels prostrate fall;
Bring forth the royal diadem, And crown Him Lord of all;
Bring forth the royal diadem, And crown Him Lord of all.

Ye chosen seed of Israel's race, Ye ransomed from the fall, Hail
Him who saves you by His grace, And crown Him Lord of all;
Hail Him who saves you by His grace, And crown Him Lord
of all.

Let ev'ry kindred, ev'ry tribe, On this terrestrial ball, To Him
all majesty ascribe, And crown Him Lord of all; To Him all
majesty ascribe, And crown Him Lord of all.

O that with yonder sacred throng We at His feet may fall!
We'll join the everlasting song, And crown Him Lord of all;
We'll join the everlasting song, And crown Him Lord of all.

Bible Study Questions

1. Read Matthew 27:27–31.
2. The "chosen seed of Israel's race" partook in this mockery of Jesus. Do you think they had any idea of what they were doing?
3. How might they have heard the words "ev'ry kindred, ev'ry tribe," from the hymn?

Personal Reflection Questions

1. Do you ascribe too little majesty to Jesus? Why or why not?
2. Can you ascribe too much majesty to Jesus? Why or why not?
3. What keeps you from worshipping Him more fully?
4. What does worshipping Jesus look like in your day-to-day life?

Prayer

Pray a prayer of repentance for at times worshipping Christ too little, and for perhaps making a mockery of His majesty by not considering the worth He is due. Ask the Holy Spirit to help you worship Christ in all circumstances and ways.

42. Love Divine, All Loves Excelling

———— ✠ ————

Words: Charles Wesley, 1707–1788
Music: John Zundel, 1815–1882

Love divine, all loves excelling, Joy of heav'n, to earth come down; Fix in us Thy humble dwelling; All Thy faithful mercies crown. Jesus, Thou art all compassion, Pure unbounded love Thou art; Visit us with Thy salvation; Enter ev'ry trembling heart.

Breathe, O breathe Thy loving Spirit, Into ev'ry troubled breast! Let us all in Thee inherit, Let us find the promised rest; Take away our bent to sinning; Alpha and Omega be; End of faith, as its beginning, Set our hearts at liberty.

Come, Almighty to deliver, Let us all Thy grace receive; Suddenly return, and never, Nevermore Thy temples leave. Thee we would be always blessing, Serve Thee as Thy hosts above, Pray, and praise Thee without ceasing, Glory in Thy perfect love.

Finish, then, Thy new creation; Pure and spotless let us be; Let us see Thy great salvation Perfectly restored in Thee: Changed from glory into glory, Till in heav'n we take our place, Till we cast our crowns before Thee, Lost in wonder, love, and praise.

Bible Study Questions

1. Read John 14:15–31.
2. Who does Jesus promise to send?
3. Where does Jesus promise the Spirit will dwell?
4. What does Jesus promise the Spirit will teach?

Personal Reflection Questions

1. Do you believe the Holy Spirit dwells within you?
2. Does that belief inform how you live life in every way?
3. If you were to really live as though the Spirit dwelt inside of you, teaching you all things, how would your daily life look different today?

Prayer

Pray a prayer of supplication to the Father, asking Him to show you more of the Holy Spirit inside of you. Ask the Holy Spirit to empower, help, and comfort you as you obey all the things He asks of you.

43. My Jesus, I Love Thee

————— ❧ —————

Words: William R. Featherston, 1846–1873
Music: Adoniram J. Gordan, 1836–1895

My Jesus, I love Thee, I know Thou art mine; For Thee, all the follies of sin I resign; My gracious Redeemer, my Savior art Thou; If ever I loved Thee, my Jesus, 'tis now.

I love Thee because Thou hast first loved me, And purchased my pardon on Calvary's tree; I love Thee for wearing the thorns on Thy brow; If ever I loved Thee, my Jesus, 'tis now.

I'll love Thee in life, I will love Thee in death, And praise Thee as long as Thou lendest me breath; And say, when the death dew lies cold on my brow; If ever I loved Thee, my Jesus, 'tis now.

In mansions of glory and endless delight, I'll ever adore Thee in heaven so bright; And singing Thy praises, before Thee I'll bow; If ever I loved Thee, my Jesus, 'tis now.

Bible Study Questions

1. Read 1 John 4:7–21.
2. Draw four columns. List all the things love is, all the places love comes from, all those who love, and all the results of love.

Personal Reflection Questions

1. Do you find yourself challenged by your four columns from 1 John 4:7–21?
2. In what ways?
3. Which ways have you failed to give or receive love as shown above?

Prayer

Pray a prayer of thanksgiving and worship to the Father for loving you first, and for sending His Son as the greatest act of love for you. Ask the Spirit for help receiving that love in fullness and showing it to others.

44. I Love Thee

———— ✢ ————

Words: Anonymous, Jeremiah Ingalls' *Christian Harmony*, 1805
Music: Anonymous, Jeremiah Ingalls' *Christian Harmony*, 1805

I love Thee, I love Thee, I love Thee, my Lord; I love Thee, my Savior, I love Thee my God: I love Thee, I love Thee, and that Thou dost know; But how much I love Thee my actions will show.

I'm happy I'm happy, oh, wondrous account! My joys are immortal, I stand on the mount: I gaze on my treasure and long to be there, With Jesus and angels and kindred so dear.

O Jesus, my Savior, with Thee I am blest, My life and salvation, my joy and my rest: Thy name by my theme, and Thy love be my song; Thy grace shall inspire both my heart and my tongue.

Oh, who's like my Savior? He's Salem's bright King; He smiles and He loves me and helps me to sing: I'll praise Him, I'll praise Him with notes loud and clear, While rivers of pleasure my spirit shall cheer.

Bible Study Questions

1. Read Matthew 13:44–46.
2. Why did Jesus compare the kingdom of God to something hidden?
3. Why did Jesus talk about the kingdom of God being like something that had to be bought?

Personal Reflection Questions

1. Do you find the treasure of the kingdom easy to find or difficult?
2. What has it cost you to have access to the kingdom of God?
3. Do you treat the kingdom of God as precious in your daily life, or do you overlook its value?

Prayer

Pray a prayer of repentance for treating the kingdom of God as though it were not a costly thing, for you or for Christ, who died on the cross for you. Ask the Spirit for help as you "sell everything you have" in order to gain the kingdom.

45. Oh, How I Love Jesus

———— ✤ ————

Words: Frederick Whitfield, 1829–1904
Music: Anonymous

There is a name I love to hear, I love to sing its worth; It sounds as music in my ear, The sweetest name on earth. Oh, how I love Jesus, Oh how I love Jesus, Oh, how I love Jesus, Because He first loved me.

It tells me of a Savior's love, Who died to set me free; It tells me of His precious blood, The sinner's perfect plea. Oh, how I love Jesus, Oh how I love Jesus, Oh, how I love Jesus, Because He first loved me.

It tells me what my Father has In store for ev'ry day; And though I tread a darksome path, Yields sunshine all the way. Oh, how I love Jesus, Oh how I love Jesus, Oh, how I love Jesus, Because He first loved me.

It tells of One whose loving heart Can fells my deepest woe,
Who in each sorrow bears a part, That none can bear below.
Oh, how I love Jesus, Oh how I love Jesus, Oh, how I love
Jesus, Because He first loved me.

Bible Study Questions

1. Read John 18:15–27 and 21:15–19.
2. Why do you think Jesus asked Peter the same question three times in chapter 21?
3. Why was Peter grieved that Jesus asked him three times?

Personal Reflection Questions

1. Do you ever feel you need to prove your love to the Lord?
2. How has Christ proved His love for you?
3. Are you ever tempted to deny Christ to others, or to deny His love for you to yourself? Why?

Prayer

Pray a prayer of supplication to the Father, asking Him for help to believe, fully, that Christ loves you and gave Himself for you. Worship Christ for His work on the cross and confess truths from Scripture about His love for you.

46. Majestic Sweetness Sits Enthroned

———— ✤ ————

Words: Samuel Stennett, 1727–1795
Music: Thomas Hastings, 1784–1872

Majestic sweetness sits enthroned Upon the Savior's brow; His head with radiant glories crowned, His lips with grace o'er- flow, His lips with grace o'erflow.

No mortal can with Him compare, Among the sons of men; Fairer is He than all the fair Who fill the heav'nly train, Who fill the heav'nly train.

He saw me plunged in deep distress, And flew to my relief; For me He bore the shameful cross, And carried all my grief, And carried all my grief.

To Him I owe my life and breath, And all the joys I have; He makes me triumph over death, And saves me from the grave, And saves me from the grave.

Bible Study Questions

1. Read Hebrews 12:1–2.
2. Why does Jesus rule from a seated place instead of a standing one?
3. Write down all the verbs in this passage. Beside each, write who does the action.

Personal Reflection Questions

1. From the passage above, what are you called to do in this life on earth?
2. What are some sins you need to lay aside? What are some weights?
3. Are you able to look at Jesus as the Author and Finisher? Does that encourage you in your walk toward Him?

Prayer

Pray a prayer of supplication to the Father, asking for the help of the Spirit as you continue to run with endurance the race marked out for you toward Jesus, who has done the hardest work already and is seated on the throne.

47. When Morning Gilds the Skies

————— ❀ —————

Words: *Katholiches Gesangbuch*, Wurzburg, 1828; st. 1, 2, 4, tr.
Edward Caswall, 1814–1878; st. 3, tr. Robert Bridges,
1844–1930
Music: Joseph Barnby, 1838–1896

*When morning gilds the skies, My heart awaking cries, May
Jesus Christ be praised! Alike at work and prayer, To Jesus I
repair; May Jesus Christ be praised.*

*The night becomes as day, When from the heart we say, May
Jesus Christ be praised! The pow'rs of darkness fear, When
this sweet song they hear, May Jesus Christ be praised.*

*Ye nations of mankind, In this your concord find: May Jesus
Christ be praised! Let all the earth around Ring joyous with
the sound: May Jesus Christ be praised.*

In heav'n's eternal bliss The loveliest strain is this, May Jesus Christ be praised! Let earth, and sea, and sky From depth to height reply, May Jesus Christ be praised.

Bible Study Questions

1. Read Ephesians 6:10–20.
2. Make a list of what God has provided armor against (schemes of the devil, rulers, etc.).

Personal Reflection Questions

1. Which of these pieces of armor feel difficult for you to "put on" each day?
2. Where do you feel vulnerable to the powers of darkness?
3. Do you believe that Christ desires to protect you from these powers of darkness?

Prayer

Pray a prayer of supplication to the Father, asking Him to protect you from all the cosmic powers over this present darkness and the schemes of the devil. Ask for the help of the Holy Spirit to wear the armor God has provided for you.

48. Praise Him! Praise Him!

———— ❧ ————

Words: Fanny J. Crosby, 1820–1915
Music: Chester G. Allen, 1838–1878

Praise Him! praise Him! Jesus, our blessed Redeemer! Sing, O earth, His wonderful love proclaim! Hail Him! hail Him! highest archangels in glory, Strength and honor give to His holy name! Like a shepherd, Jesus will guard His children; In His arms He carries them all day long: Praise Him! praise Him! tell of His excellent greatness! Praise Him! praise Him! ever in joyful song!

Praise Him! praise Him! Jesus, our blessed Redeemer! For our sins, He suffered and bled and died; He our Rock, our hope of eternal salvation, Hail Him! hail Him! Jesus the crucified: Sound His praises! Jesus who bore our sorrows, Love unbounded, wonderful, deep, and strong: Praise Him! praise Him! tell of His excellent greatness! Praise Him! praise Him! ever in joyful song!

Praise Him! praise Him! Jesus, our blessed Redeemer! Heav'nly portals loud with hosannas ring! Jesus, Savior, Reigneth forever and ever; Crown Him! crown Him! prophet and priest and King! Christ is coming, over the world victorious, Pow'r and glory unto the Lord belong: Praise Him! praise Him! tell of His excellent greatness! Praise Him! praise Him! ever in joyful song!

Bible Study Questions

1. Read Isaiah 66:15–24.
2. Who does this passage say will worship the Lord?
3. Who will not?

Personal Reflection Questions

1. Do you believe that all will confess Jesus as Lord?
2. Are there those whom you believe are beyond the grace of God?
3. What would it look like for you to communicate Christ and the gospel to them?

Prayer

Pray a prayer of confession and repentance for believing or acting like anyone could be beyond the grace of God. Pray earnestly for the salvation of someone you know or know about.

49. Bless That Wonderful Name

———— ✤ ————

Words: Traditional African American
Music: Traditional African American

Bless that wonderful name of Jesus, Bless that wonderful name of Jesus, Bless that wonderful name of Jesus, No other name I know.

Sing that wonderful name of Jesus, Sing that wonderful name of Jesus, Sing that wonderful name of Jesus, No other name I know.

Preach that wonderful name of Jesus, Preach that wonderful name of Jesus, Preach that wonderful name of Jesus, No other name I know.

Praise that wonderful name of Jesus, Praise that wonderful name of Jesus, Praise that wonderful name of Jesus, No other name I know.

Share that wonderful name of Jesus, Share that wonderful name of Jesus, Share that wonderful name of Jesus, No other name I know.

Bible Study Questions

1. Read Acts 4.
2. What "other names" might the council have wanted Peter and John to say men might be saved by?
3. Why was it important to clarify that there was no other name but one by which men could be saved?

Personal Reflection Questions

1. What things/places/people do you run to for comfort, healing, hope, etc.?
2. Do you find those things/places/people fulfilling for long?
3. Where is your truest and most lasting hope?

Prayer

Pray a prayer of repentance to the Father for running to other things to find living water. Ask the Spirit to help you as you endeavor to know only one name: the name of Christ.

50. Pentecostal Power

———— ❖ ————

Words: Charles H. Gabriel, 1856–1932
Music: Charles H. Gabriel, 1856–1932

Lord, as of old at Pentecost Thou didst Thy pow'r display, With cleansing, purifying flame, Descend on us today. Lord, send the old-time power, the Pentecostal power! Thy floodgates of blessing on us throw open wide! Lord, send the old-time power, the Pentecostal power, That sinners be converted and Thy name glorified!

For mighty works for Thee, prepare And strengthen ev'ry heart; Come, take possession of Thine own, And never-more depart. Lord, send the old-time power, the Pentecostal power, That sinners be converted and Thy name glorified!

All self consume, all sin destroy! With earnest zeal endue Each waiting heart to work for Thee; O Lord, our faith renew! Lord, send the old-time power, the Pentecostal power, That sinners be converted and Thy name glorified!

Speak, Lord! before Thy throne we wait, Thy promise we believe, And will not let Thee go until The blessing we receive. Lord, send the old-time power, the Pentecostal power, That sinners be converted and Thy name glorified!

Bible Study Questions

1. Read Acts 2.
2. What expressions of the Holy Spirit happened on this day?
3. What expressions of the Holy Spirit are still happening today?

Personal Reflection Questions

1. How do you understand the role of the Holy Spirit in your life and the Church today?
2. In what ways is the Holy Spirit empowering and helping the Church to usher in Christ's coming?
3. In what ways do you doubt or question the way the Holy Spirit is talked about or utilized today?
4. What does Scripture say to your specific questions or doubts?

Prayer

Pray a prayer of supplication to the Father, asking Him to reveal the truths of the Holy Spirit to you, asking for help, empowerment, comfort, and wisdom from above.

51. Spirit of God, Descend upon My Heart

Words: George Croly, 1780–1860
Music: Frederick C. Atkinson, 1841–1897

Spirit of God, descend upon my heart; Wean it from earth; Thro' all its pulses move; Stoop to my weakness, mighty as Thou art, And make me love Thee as I ought to love.

I ask no dream, no prophet ecstasies, No sudden rending of the veil of clay, No angel visitant, no op'nig skies; But take the dimness of my soul away.

Teach me to feel that Thou art always nigh; Teach me the struggles of the soul to bear. To check the rising doubt, the rebel sigh; Teach me the patience of unceasing prayer.

Teach me to love Thee as Thine angels love, One holy passion filling all my frame; The kindling of the heav'n descended Dove, My heart an alter, and Thy love the flame.

Bible Study Questions

1. Read Matthew 22:34–40.
2. How was the lawyer's question a test?
3. How was the answer Jesus gave satisfactory?

Personal Reflection Questions

1. How does the Holy Spirit change your heart? Your soul? Your mind?
2. Which of these three areas are you most reluctant to let the Spirit change?
3. Why? What would you lose if you were to be deeply changed in this part of your being?

Prayer

Pray a prayer of worship to the Father for sending the Holy Spirit. Ask the Spirit to change you completely, from old to new, from broken to whole. Ask for comfort, help, joy, and fullness.

52. Come, Thou Almighty King

——— ❧ ———

Words: Anonymous
Music: Felice de Giardini, 1716–1796

Come, Thou Almighty King, Help us Thy name to sing, Help us to praise: Father, all glorious, O'er all victorious, Come and reign over us, Ancient of Days.

Come, Thou Incarnate Word, Gird on Thy mighty sword, Our prayer attend! Come, and Thy people bless, And give Thy word success: Spirit of holiness, On us descent.

Come, Holy Comforter, Thy sacred witness bear In this glad hour! Thou, who almighty art, Now rule in ev'ry heart And ne'er from us depart, Spirit of pow'r.

To Thee, great One in Three, The highest praises be, Hence evermore; Thy sov'reign majesty May we in glory see, And to eternity Love and adore.

Bible Study Questions

1. Read Daniel 7.
2. Why did Daniel keep the matter in his heart (v. 28)?
3. How might the original hearers have heard and interpreted this passage?

Personal Reflection Questions

1. Christ was both meek and King, humble and almighty, flesh and sovereign. How do these seeming dichotomies help you worship Him more?
2. Do you feel more weak or strong generally?
3. How does knowing Christ fully embodied both encourage or challenge you today?

Prayer

Pray a prayer of confession and supplication. Confess your weakness before the King. Ask the Spirit for help as you grow in strength and stay mindful of Christ's perfect strength.

53. Wonderful Words of Life

———— ✛ ————

Words: Philip P. Bliss, 1838–1876
Music: Philip P. Bliss, 1838–1876

Sing, them over again to me, Wonderful words of life; Let me more of their beauty see, Wonderful words of life; Words of life and beauty, Teach me faith and duty: Beautiful words, wonderful words, Wonderful words of life; Beautiful words, wonderful words, Wonderful words of life.

Christ, the blessed One, gives to all Wonderful words of life; Sinner, list to the loving call, Wonderful words of life; All so freely given, Wooing us to heaven: Beautiful words, wonderful words, Wonderful words of life; Beautiful words, wonderful words, Wonderful words of life.

Sweetly echo the gospel call, Wonderful words of life; Offer pardon and peace to all, Wonderful words of life; Jesus, only Savior, Sanctify forever, Beautiful words, wonderful words,

Wonderful words of life; Beautiful words, wonderful words,
Wonderful words of life.

Bible Study Questions

1. Read Proverbs 16:20–33.
2. Circle all the times the words *lips, instruct, teach, whisper,* and *mouth* appear.

Personal Reflection Questions

1. The Bible says death and life are in the power of the tongue (Proverbs 18:21). Do you use your tongue more for death or life? For building up or tearing down?
2. If Jesus has the "wonderful words of life," how do the words of your mouth reflect that?
3. What would it look like to embrace and embody "wonderful words of life" as you go through your day?

Prayer

Pray a prayer of repentance to the Father for using your tongue for evil instead of for good. Ask for the help of the Spirit to fill your mouth with words that glorify the Father and bring joy to others.

54. Dear Lord and Father of Mankind

———— ❧ ————

Words: John Greenleaf Whittier, 1807–1892
Music: Frederick C. Maker, 1844–1927

*Dear Lord and Father of mankind, Forgive our foolish ways;
Reclothe us in our rightful mind; In purer lives Thy service
find, In deeper rev'rence praise.*

*Drop Thy still dews of quietness, Till all our strivings cease;
Take from our souls the strain and stress, And let our ordered
lives confess The beauty of Thy peace.*

*Breathe thro' the heats of our desire Thy coolness and Thy
balm; Let sense be dumb, let flesh retire; Speak thro' the
earthquake, wind, and fire, O still small voice of calm!*

*In simple trust like theirs who heard, Beside the Syrian sea,
The gracious calling of the Lord, Let us, like them, without a
word, Rise up and follow Thee.*

Bible Study Questions

1. Read Philippians 4.
2. What was Paul's encouragement to the believers in Philippi who had conflict and discord among them?
3. What does "the peace of God, which passeth all understanding" mean (v. 7)?

Personal Reflection Questions

1. Do you often feel as though you need all the information available before you can feel at peace? Why?
2. Do you often feel as though you must be fully understood before you can have peace? Why?
3. How do this hymn and this passage from Scripture speak directly to your heart and mind today?

Prayer

Pray a prayer of confession and repentance to the Father for thinking you or others need to know everything about a situation in order to have peace. Ask for the peace of Christ to guard your heart and mind today.

55. I Lay My Sins on Jesus

———— ✦ ————

Words: Horatius Bonar, 1808–1889
Music: Samuel S. Wesley, 1810–1876

I lay my sins on Jesus, The spotless Lamb of God; He bears them all, and frees us From the accursed load: I bring my guilt to Jesus, To wash my crimson stains White in His blood most precious Till not a stain remains.

I lay my wants on Jesus; All fullness dwells in Him; He heals all my diseases, He doth my soul redeem: I lay my griefs on Jesus, My burdens and my cares; He from them all releases, He all my sorrows shares.

I long to be like Jesus, Strong, loving, lowly, mild; I long to be like Jesus, The Father's holy child: I long to be with Jesus, Amid the heav'nly throng, To sing with saints His praises, To learn the angels' song.

Bible Study Questions

1. Read 1 Peter 5:6–11.
2. What does man do in this passage? What does the enemy do? What does God do?

Personal Reflection Questions

1. Does it more often seem like God is prowling around waiting to devour you when you feel anxious or worried or prideful? Why do you think that is?
2. What is the posture of God in this passage? How does He care for you specifically?
3. What does it look like for you to "humble [yourself] . . . under the mighty hand of God" (v. 6)?

Prayer

Pray a prayer of supplication, asking the Father to give you the strength to lay your concerns, anxiety, pride, and all else at His throne, knowing He cares for you.

56. I Surrender All

———— ✠ ————

Words: Judson W. Van DeVenter, 1855–1939
Music: Winfield S. Weeden, 1847–1908

All to Jesus I surrender, All to Him I freely give; I will ever love and trust Him, In His presence daily live. I surrender all, I surrender all; All to Thee, my blessed Savior, I surrender all.

All to Jesus I surrender, Make me, Savior, wholly Thine; Let me feel Thy Holy Spirit, Truly know that Thou art mine. I surrender all, I surrender all; All to Thee, my blessed Savior, I surrender all.

All to Jesus I surrender, Lord, I give myself to Thee; Fill me with Thy love and power, Let Thy blessing fall on me. I surrender all, I surrender all; All to Thee, my blessed Savior, I surrender all.

Bible Study Questions

1. Read 1 Corinthians 9.
2. List all the things or ways Paul surrendered his rights, freedoms, outcomes, and comforts.
3. For what sake does Paul say he surrendered?

Personal Reflection Questions

1. Do you willingly surrender your rights, freedoms, outcomes, and comforts?
2. What is something that is difficult for you to surrender?
3. What do you have to lose by surrendering this right, freedom, outcome, or comfort to Jesus?

Prayer

Pray a prayer of confession and repentance to the Father for the ways you have tried to remain the lord of your own life. Ask the Spirit for help as you surrender your perceived rights, freedoms, outcomes, and comforts to the Lord.

57. O Jesus, I Have Promised

Words: John E. Bode, 1816–1874
Music: Arthur H. Mann, 1850–1929

O Jesus, I have promised To serve Thee to the end; Be Thou forever near me, My Master and my friend; I shall not fear the battle If Thou art by my side, Nor wander from the pathway If Thou wilt be my guide.

O Jesus, Thou hast promised To all who follow Thee, That where Thou art in glory, There shall Thy servant be; And, Jesus, I have promised To serve Thee to the end; O give me grace to follow My Master and my friend!

O let me feel Thee near me! The world is ever near; I see the sights that dazzle, The tempting sounds I hear; My foes are ever near me, Around me and within; But, Jesus, draw Thou nearer And shield my soul from sin.

O let me hear Thee speaking In accents clear and still, Above the storms of passion, The murmurs of self-will. O speak to reassure me, To hasten or control! O speak, and make me listen, Thou guardian of my soul!

Bible Study Questions

1. Read John 14.
2. What does Jesus promise in this passage? List all His promises.
3. What is required of man in this passage?

Personal Reflection Questions

1. What are some things that God has not promised to give but you act as though He has (money, health, fame, bigger house, better car, marriage, happiness, etc.)?
2. What is your posture toward God when you feel He hasn't given you what you want (but what He hasn't promised)?
3. Do you trust God is faithful to Himself and to His Word?

Prayer

Pray a prayer of worship and adoration to the Father for being one who gives perfect gifts and for being faithful to His name. Praise Him for always honoring His Word and always giving us what is best, even if it doesn't seem best to us.

58. Take My Life, and Let It Be Consecrated

———— ❖ ————

Words: Frances R. Havergal, 1836–1879
Music: Henri A. Malan, 1787–1864; harm. Lowell Mason, 1792–1872

Take my life and let it be Consecrated, Lord to Thee; Take my hands and let them move At the impulse of Thy love, At the impulse of Thy love.

Take my feet and let them be Swift and beautiful for Thee; Take my voice and let me sing Always, only, for my King, Always, only for my King.

Take my silver and my gold, Not a mite would I withhold; Take my moments and my days, Let them flow in ceaseless praise, Let them flow in ceaseless praise.

Take my will and make it Thine, It shall be no longer mine; Take my heart, it is Thine own, It shall be Thy royal throne, It shall be Thy royal throne.

Bible Study Questions

1. Read Genesis 22.
2. What was Abraham's response to God's command? How quickly did he move to obey?
3. What does this say about Abraham's trust in God?

Personal Reflection Questions

1. Has there been a time when you have refused to give God what He was asking of you? Why?
2. Did you still end up having to give up the thing you wanted to keep, even unwillingly?
3. Looking back, where do you see the Lord's faithfulness to Himself and to you in that time?

Prayer

Pray a prayer of thanksgiving to the Father for always caring for you, even when you didn't care to listen to Him. Ask the Spirit for help as you give up your rights and freedoms, and entrust your life to the God who loves you.

59. O Master, Let Me Walk with Thee

———— ✤ ————

Words: Washington Gladden, 1836–1918
Music: H. Percy Smith, 1825–1898

O Master, let me walk with Thee In lowly paths of service free; Tell me Thy secret, help me bear The strain of toil, the fret of care.

Help me the slow of heart to move By some clear, winning word of love; Teach me the wayward feet to stay, And guide them I the homeward way.

Teach me Thy patience; still with Thee In closer, dearer company, In work that keeps faith sweet and strong, In trust that triumphs over wrong.

In hope that sends a shining ray Far down the future's broad'ing way, In peace that only Thou canst give, With Thee, O Master, let me live.

Bible Study Questions

1. Read Luke 5.
2. What do you think the first disciples thought when the Master called them in that moment?
3. Do you think the disciples envisioned the life of loss ahead of them, with gains only found in eternity?

Personal Reflection Questions

1. What has been the cost of walking with the Lord for you?
2. Do you trust that the Lord sees those very real losses and mourns with you over them?
3. What is something the Lord is asking you to walk away from today?

Prayer

Pray a prayer of supplication, asking the Father to help you as you give over your livelihood, your security, your reputation, or whatever He is asking you to relinquish to Him today. Ask the Holy Spirit to comfort you in the losses and remind you of eternity to come.

60. I Saw the Cross of Jesus

———— ✠ ————

Words: Frederick Whitfield, 1829–1904
Music: Anonymous

I saw the cross of Jesus, When burdened with my sin; I sought the cross of Jesus, To give me peace within; I brought my soul to Jesus, He cleansed it in His blood; And in the cross of Jesus I found my peace with God.

I love the cross of Jesus, It tells me what I am—A vile and guilty creature, Saved only thro' the Lamb; In ev'ry fear and conflict, I more than conqueror am; Living, I'm safe, or dying, Thro' Christ, the risen Lamb.

Safe in the cross of Jesus! There let my weary heart Still rest in peace unshaken, Till with Him, Ne'er to part; And then in strains of glory I'll sing His wondrous pow'r, Where sin can never enter, And death is known no more.

Bible Study Questions

1. Read Romans 8.
2. Make lists of all the things the law is, man is, the Spirit is, and Christ did.

Personal Reflection Questions

1. Using the list above, in what ways have you tried through the law to gain the approval of God?
2. In what ways have you tried to accomplish the work of the Spirit or Christ in your own life?
3. How does Romans 8 assure and comfort you in the finished work of Christ and the ongoing work of the Spirit?

Prayer

Pray a prayer of worship and adoration to the Father for sending His Son and giving you His Spirit as a comforter and helper. Thank the Son for fulfilling the law and doing what you could not do.

61. I Am Thine, O Lord

———— ❧ ————

Words: Fanny J. Crosby, 1820–1915
Music: William H. Doane, 1832–1915

I am Thine, O Lord, I have heard Thy voice, And it told Thy love to me; But I long to rise in the arms of faith, And be closer drawn to Thee. Draw me nearer, nearer, blessed Lord, To the cross where Thou hast died; Draw me nearer, nearer, nearer, blessed Lord, To Thy precious, bleeding side.

Consecrate me now to Thy service, Lord, By the pow'r of grace divine; Let my soul look up with a steadfast hope, And my will be lost in Thine. Draw me nearer, nearer, blessed Lord, To the cross where Thou hast died; Draw me nearer, nearer, nearer, blessed Lord, To Thy precious, bleeding side.

O the pure delight of a single hour That before Thy throne I spend; When I kneel in prayer, and with Thee, my God, I commune as friend with friend! Draw me nearer, nearer, blessed

Lord, To the cross where Thou hast died; Draw me nearer, nearer, nearer, blessed Lord, To Thy precious, bleeding side.

There are depths of love that I cannot know Till I cross the narrow sea; There are heights of joy that I may not reach Till I rest in peace with Thee. Draw me nearer, nearer, blessed Lord, To the cross where Thou hast died; Draw me nearer, nearer, nearer, blessed Lord, To Thy precious, bleeding side.

Bible Study Questions

1. Read Hebrews 7 and 10.
2. Circle the phrases *draw near or draw nigh* in both the verses and the hymn.
3. How do you think the Hebrews would have understood the concept of "drawing near" in their culture and historic religious practices?

Personal Reflection Questions

1. Do you know you can draw near to God? Do you feel like He draws near to you?
2. What keeps you at a distance from God?
3. Are there sins or incorrect beliefs about God you need to repent of?

Prayer

Pray a prayer of confession and repentance to the Father for holding yourself back from Him. Ask Him to draw near to you as you draw near to Him.

62. Pass Me Not, O Gentle Savior

———— ✦ ————

Words: Fanny J. Crosby, 1820–1915
Music: William H. Doane, 1832–1915

Pass me not, O gentle Savior, Hear my humble cry; While on others Thou art calling, Do not pass me by. Savior, Savior, Hear my humble cry; While on others Thou art calling, Do not pass me by.

Let me at Thy throne of mercy Find a sweet relief; Kneeling there in deep contrition, Help my unbelief. Savior, Savior, Hear my humble cry; While on others Thou art calling, Do not pass me by.

Trusting only in Thy merit, Would I seek Thy face; Heal my wounded, broken spirit, Save me by Thy grace. Savior, Savior, Hear my humble cry; While on others Thou art calling, Do not pass me by.

Thou the spring of all my comfort, More than life to me, Whom have I on earth beside Thee? Whom in heav'n but Thee? Savior, Savior, Hear my humble cry; While on others Thou art calling, Do not pass me by.

Bible Study Questions

1. Read Psalm 73 out loud slowly, letting God's Word comfort and convict you as you read.

Personal Reflection Questions

1. As you read Psalm 73 out loud, did the Lord comfort or convict you in any areas?
2. What would it look like for you to take action on the areas of conviction that were brought to mind?
3. What would it look like for you to truly receive the comfort of the Holy Spirit you were reminded of?

Prayer

Pray a prayer of supplication to the Father, asking for the continual comfort and conviction of the Holy Spirit in your life. Ask the Spirit to remind you of His presence continually.

63. Out of My Bondage, Sorrow, and Night

———— ✠ ————

Words: William T. Sleeper, 1819–1904
Music: George C. Stebbins, 1846–1945

Out of my bondage, sorrow, and night, Jesus, I come, Jesus, I come; Into Thy freedom, gladness, and light, Jesus, I come to Thee; Out of my sickness into Thy health, Out of my want and into Thy wealth, Out of my sin and into Thyself, Jesus, I come to Thee.

Out of my shameful failure, and low, Jesus, I come, Jesus, I come; Into the glorious gain of Thy cross, Jesus, I come to Thee. Out of earth's sorrows into Thy balm, Out of life's storms and into Thy calm, Out of distress to jubilant psalm, Jesus, I come to Thee.

Out of unrest and arrogant pride, Jesus, I come, Jesus, I come; Into Thy blessed will to abide, Jesus, I come to Thee. Out of myself to dwell in Thy love, Out of despair into raptures above, Upward for aye on wings like a dove, Jesus, I come to Thee.

Out of the fear and dread of the tomb, Jesus, I come, Jesus, I come; Into the joy and light of Thy home, Jesus, I come to Thee. Out of the depths of ruin untold, Into the peace of Thy sheltering fold, Ever Thy glorious face to behold, Jesus, I come to Thee.

Bible Study Questions

1. Read Mark 2:1–12.
2. What did it require of the lame man for him to see Jesus?
3. What did it require of his friends?
4. What did it require of Jesus?
5. What did it require of the crowd?

Personal Reflection Questions

1. When you have desired healing or freedom in an area, have you considered the cost of getting it?
2. Why do you think this passage from Mark 2 is so important for us to read today?

3. What is a cost you're being asked to pay in order to see healing of your own or someone else's?

Prayer

Pray a prayer of supplication, asking the Father to draw you or others out of paralyzing sickness of some sort, whether it's blindness, fear, anxiety, pride, or habitual sin. Ask the Spirit for help as you walk in obedience to the cost.

64. Jesus Is Tenderly Calling

———— ❧ ————

Words: Fanny J. Crosby, 1820–1915
Music: George C. Stebbins, 1846–1945

Jesus is tenderly calling thee home, Calling today, calling today; Why from the sunshine of love wilt thou roam Father and father away? Calling today, Calling today; Jesus is calling, Is tenderly calling today.

Jesus is calling the weary to rest, Calling today, calling today; Bring Him thy burden and thou shalt be blest; He will not turn thee away. Calling today, Calling today; Jesus is calling, Is tenderly calling today.

Jesus is waiting; O come to Him now, Waiting today, waiting today; Come with thy sins; at His feet lowly bow; Come, and no longer delay. Calling today, Calling today; Jesus is calling, Is tenderly calling today.

Jesus is pleading; O list to His voice, Hear Him today, hear Him today; They who believe on His name shall rejoice; Quickly arise and away. Calling today, Calling today; Jesus is calling, Is tenderly calling today.

Bible Study Questions

1. Read Mark 10:46–52.
2. Why do you think Jesus didn't call for the man Himself?
3. Do you think the blind man would have recognized the voice of Jesus?

Personal Reflection Questions

1. Has there been a time in your life when someone else had to tell you the truth about Scripture or God's character, even when you could have read or known it yourself?
2. Why did you hear better when it came through the voice of another?
3. What truth from Scripture might the Lord be asking you to share with someone today? Will you be obedient to do it?

Prayer

Pray a prayer of worship to the Father for sending messengers of His grace to you, real, live voices full of reminders, truths, and encouragement. Ask the Spirit for help as you in turn call to others using the Word of God and truths of Scripture.

65. Send the Light

———— ✤✤ ————

Words: Charles H. Gabriel, 1856–1932
Music: Charles H. Gabriel, 1856–1932

There's a call comes ringing o'er the restless wave, "Send the light! Send the light!" There are souls to rescue, there are souls to save, Send the light! Send the light! Send the light! the blessed gospel light; Let it shine from shore to shore, shine forevermore!

We have heard the Macedonian call today, "Send the light! Send the light!" And a golden off'ring at the cross we lay, Send the light! Send the light! Send the light, the blessed gospel light; Let it shine from shore to shore! shine forevermore!

Let us pray that grace may ev'rywhere abound, "Send the light! Send the light!" And a Christ-like spirit ev'rywhere be found, Send the light! Send the light! Send the light, the blessed gospel light; Let it shine from shore to shore! shine forevermore!

Let us not grow weary in the work of love, "Send the light!
Send the light!" Let us gather jewels for a crown above, Send
the light! Send the light! Send the light, the blessed gospel
light; Let it shine from shore to shore! shine forevermore!

Bible Study Questions

1. Read Matthew 28:16–20.
2. Why do you think God tells us in this passage that some worshipped and some doubted?

Personal Reflection Questions

1. What are some ways you've grown weary in the work of spreading the gospel?
2. How does envisioning unreached places as darkness in need of light encourage you not to grow weary?
3. Is Christ surprised by your weariness or others' doubts? What is His response to both?

Prayer

Pray a prayer of supplication, asking the Father to reignite a desire to spread the mission of Christ, to teach, disciple, and see the ends of the earth come to know Him.

66. Hark, the Voice of Jesus Calling

———— ✢ ————

Words: Daniel March, 1816–1909
Music: Attr. Wolfgang A. Mozart, 1756–1791

Hark, the voice of Jesus calling, "Who will go and work today? Fields are white, and harvests waiting, Who will bear the sheaves away?" Loud and long the Master calls us, Rich reward He offers free; Who will answer, gladly saying, "Here am I, send me, send me"?

If you cannot cross the ocean, And the distant lands explore, You can find the lost around you, You can help them at your door; If you cannot give your thousands, You can give the widow's mite; What you truly give for Jesus Will be precious in His sight.

Let none hear you idly saying, "There is nothing I can do," While the lost of earth are dying, And the Master calls for you; Take the task He give you gladly; Let His work your pleasure be; Answer quickly when He calls, "Here am I, send me, send me."

Bible Study Questions

1. Read John 4:1–45.
2. What does Jesus mean when He says His food is to do the will of the one who sent Him (v. 34)?
3. Why does Jesus talk about food immediately after ministering to the woman at the well and right before many came to Him seeking His ministry? What does this tell you about the message of Jesus?

Personal Reflection Questions

1. Do you feel satisfied in the work of the gospel?
2. If all you were called to do, for all of life, was to be faithful with small things, to minister in your limited capacity, would it be food enough for you?
3. Why or why not?

Prayer

Pray a prayer of thanksgiving to the Father for placing you in the right places at the right times in order to see His work advance. Ask Him for the strength to be faithful with today.

67. Jesus Shall Reign

———— ✤ ————

Words: Isaac Watts, 1674–1748
Music: John Hatton, c. 1710–1793

Jesus shall reign where'er the sun Does its successive journeys run; His kingdom spread from shore to shore, Till moons shall wax and wane no more.

To Him shall endless pray'r be made, And endless praises crown His head; His name like sweet perfume shall rise With ev'ry morning sacrifice.

People and realms of ev'ry tongue Dwell on His love with sweetest song, And infant voices shall proclaim Their early blessings on His name.

Let ev'ry creature rise and bring Honor and glory to our King; Angels descend with songs again, And earth repeat the loud "Amen!"

Bible Study Questions

1. Read Philippians 2:1–11.
2. How many will bow and how many tongues will confess Jesus is Lord?

Personal Reflection Questions

1. How does the knowledge that every single human who has ever lived or who ever will live will bow before Christ, confessing Him as Lord, change how you view areas of rebellion in your heart?
2. How does it change how you view areas of rebellion in others?
3. Does it comfort you that all will bow and all will confess?

Prayer

Pray a prayer of supplication to the Father. Ask Him to change hearts around you, and to change your heart too, leaving nothing untouched for His glory.

68. We've a Story to Tell

———— ✤ ————

Words: H. Ernest Nichol, 1862–1926
Music: H. Ernest Nichol, 1862–1926

We've a story to tell to the nations, That shall turn their hearts to the right, A story of truth and mercy, A story of peace and light, A story of peace and light. For the darkness shall turn to dawning, And the dawning to noon-day bright, And Christ's great kingdom shall come to earth, The kingdom of love and light.

We've a song to be sung to the nations, That shall lift their hearts to the Lord, A song that shall conquer evil, And show us that God is love, And show us that God is love. For the darkness shall turn to dawning, And the dawning to noon-day bright, And Christ's great kingdom shall come to earth, The kingdom of love and light.

We've a message to give to the nations, That the Lord who reigneth above Hath sent us His Son to save us, And show us that God is love, And show us that God is love. For the darkness shall turn to dawning, And the dawning to noon-day bright, And Christ's great kingdom shall come to earth, The kingdom of love and light.

We've a Savior to show to the nations, Who the path of sorrow hath trod, That all of the world's great peoples May come to the truth of God, May come to the truth of God! For the darkness shall turn to dawning, And the dawning to noon-day bright, And Christ's great kingdom shall come to earth, The kingdom of love and light.

Bible Study Questions

1. Read Matthew 6:5–15.
2. Why did Jesus tell His followers to pray for His kingdom to come *on earth* as it is in heaven?
3. How might His original hearers have interpreted His words?

Personal Reflection Questions

1. What do you envision it to look like for Christ's kingdom to come on earth?

2. In what ways do you see Christ's kingdom being established today around you?

3. Do you feel more hopeful or hopeless when you think about the future of our earth, the nations, and eternity?

Prayer

Pray a prayer of adoration and worship that Christ has never once left the world and everything in it to the devices of the enemy. Praise Him for caring and coming, and grow more excited about establishing His kingdom upon all the earth.

69. O Zion, Haste

———— ✤ ————

Words: Mary Ann Thomson, 1834–1923
Music: James Walch, 1837–1901

O Zion, haste, thy mission high fulfilling, To tell to all the world that God is Light; That He who made all nations is not willing One soul should perish, lost in shades of night. Publish glad tidings, tidings of peace, Tidings of Jesus, redemption and release.

Behold how many thousands still are lying Bound in the darksome prisonhouse of sin, With non to tell them of the Savior's dying, Or of the life He died for them to win. Publish glad tidings, tidings of peace, Tidings of Jesus, redemption and release.

Proclaim to ev'ry people, tongue, and nation That God, in whom they live and move, is Love: Tell how He stoop'd to save His lost creation, And died on earth that we might live above. Publish glad tidings, tidings of peace, Tidings of Jesus, redemption and release.

Give of thy sons to bear the message glorious; Give of thy wealth to speed them on their way; Pour out thy soul for them in pray'r victorious; And all thou spendest Jesus will repay. Publish glad tidings, tidings of peace, Tidings of Jesus, redemption and release.

Bible Study Questions

1. Read John 3:1–21.
2. How do you think Nicodemus, the Pharisee, would have heard and interpreted the words of Jesus about loving or hating the light?
3. Do you think he would have thought he was a light-lover?

Personal Reflection Questions

1. What are some areas in your life where you have hated the light, when you have pressed away from correction or challenge?
2. What are areas in your life where you have tried to walk in the light?

3. Do you feel more condemned by those areas still in the darkness or those in the light?
4. What do you need to believe about Christ or yourself today in order to walk free from condemnation?

Prayer

Pray a prayer of repentance for the areas in your life in which you walk in and love the darkness more than light. Ask the Father for help as you endeavor to walk in the light, in freedom from condemnation.

70. We Have Heard the Joyful Sound

———— ❧ ————

Words: Priscilla Owens, 1829–1907
Music: William J. Kirkpatrick, 1838–1921

*We have heard the joyful sound: Jesus saves! Jesus saves!
Spread the tidings all around: Jesus saves! Jesus saves! Bear
the news to ev'ry land, Climb the steep and cross the waves;
Onward! 'tis our Lord's command; Jesus saves! Jesus saves!*

*Waft it on the rolling tide: Jesus saves! Jesus saves! Tell to sin-
ners far and wide: Jesus saves! Jesus saves! Sing, ye islands
of the sea; Echo back, ye ocean caves; Earth shall keep her
jubilee: Jesus saves! Jesus saves!*

*Sing above the battle strife: Jesus saves! Jesus saves! By His
death and endless life Jesus saves! Jesus saves! Sing it softly
thro' the gloom, When the heart for mercy craves; Sing in triumph o'er the tomb: Jesus saves! Jesus saves!*

Give the winds a mighty voice: Jesus saves! Jesus saves! Let the nations now rejoice: Jesus saves! Jesus saves! Shout salvation full and free: Highest hills and deepest caves; This our song of victory: Jesus saves! Jesus saves!

Bible Study Questions

1. Read Hebrews 7:11–28.
2. What is the writer of Hebrews trying to show the readers in this passage?
3. How might the original hearers have heard "save them to the uttermost" (v. 25)?

Personal Reflection Questions

1. Do you believe Jesus saves but you must do a good amount of sanctification before He will really accept you?
2. In what ways are you like the priests of old, going back again and again to get it right with God?
3. What does this passage in Hebrews say to you about your efforts?

Prayer

Pray a prayer of adoration to God for sending His Son to save you to the uttermost, for always living to make intercession on your behalf. Rest in the truths of this gospel element.

71. I Will Sing of My Redeemer

Words: Philip P. Bliss, 1838–1876
Music: James McGranahan, 1840–1907

I will sing of my redeemer And His wondrous love to me; On the cruel cross He suffers From the curse to set me free. Sing, oh, sing of my Redeemer, With His blood He purchased me; On the cross He sealed my pardon, Paid the debt and made me free.

I will tell the wondrous story, How my lost estate to save, In His boundless love and mercy, He the ransom freely gave. Sing, oh, sing of my Redeemer, With His blood He purchased me; On the cross He sealed my pardon, Paid the debt and made me free.

I will praise my dear Redeemer, His triumphant pow'r I'll tell, How the victory He giveth Over sin and death and hell. Sing, oh, sing of my Redeemer, With His blood He purchased me;

On the cross He sealed my pardon, Paid the debt and made me free.

I will sing of my Redeemer, And His heav'nly love to me; He from death to life hath brought me, Son of God, with Him to be. Sing, oh, sing of my Redeemer, With His blood He purchased me; On the cross He sealed my pardon, Paid the debt and made me free.

Bible Study Questions

1. Read Colossians 2:6–15.
2. What does Paul mean by being circumcised by a circumcision and not by hands?
3. What legal demands did the law have against those to whom Paul was writing?

Personal Reflection Questions

1. Do you believe the gospel that saved you is the same gospel that sustains you?
2. Do you live that way? Or do you try to earn your way into a canceled debt?
3. What might today look like if you were to live as though the debt were canceled?

Prayer

Pray a prayer of confession to the Father for all the ways you have tried to earn your way into His favor and by so doing have made a mockery of the work Christ finished with His life, death, and resurrection.

72. Soldiers of Christ, in Truth Arrayed

---- ❧ ----

Words: Basil Manly Jr., 1825–1892
Music: German Melody

Soldiers of Christ, in truth arrayed, A world in ruins needs your aid: A world by sun destroyed and dead; A world for which the Savior bled.

His gospel to the lost proclaim, Good news for all in Jesus' name; Let light upon the darkness break That sinners from their death may wake.

Morning and evening sow the seed, God's grace the effort shall succeed. Seedtimes of tears have oft been found With sheaves of joy and plenty crowned.

We meet to part, but part to meet When earthly labors are complete, To join in yet more blest employ, In an eternal world of joy.

Bible Study Questions

1. Read Ephesians 2:1–10.
2. What "good works" have been prepared for followers of Christ in light of this passage?

Personal Reflection Questions

1. How does knowing you are Christ's workmanship created for good works change how you view the monotony of your day and sometimes your life?
2. What do you sense God wants to do through you today?
3. Will you be obedient to His Spirit working in you?

Prayer

Pray a prayer of thanksgiving to the Father for sending the Holy Spirit to live inside of you, leading you into all truth, guiding you and helping you do the good works that have been prepared for you before time.

73. I Love to Tell the Story

———— ✤✤ ————

Words: Katherine Hankey, 1834–1911
Music: William G. Fischer, 1835–1912

I love to tell the story Of unseen things above, Of Jesus and His glory, Of Jesus and His love: I love to tell the story Because I know 'tis true; It satisfies my longings As nothing else can do. I love to tell the story, 'Twill be my theme in glory To tell the old, old story of Jesus and His love.

I love to tell the story; 'Tis pleasant to repeat What seems each time I tell it, More wonderfully sweet: I love to tell the story, For some have never heard The message of salvation From God's own holy Word. I love to tell the story, 'Twill be my theme in glory To tell the old, old story of Jesus and His love.

I love to tell the story; For those who know it best Seem hungering and thirsting To hear it, like the rest: And when, in scenes of glory, I sing the new, new song. 'Twill be the old, old story

That I have loved so long. I love to tell the story, 'Twill be my theme in glory To tell the old, old story of Jesus and His love.

Bible Study Questions

1. Read Matthew 28.
2. What story in verse 15 has been spread throughout the Jews until this day?
3. What other story has been spread throughout the whole world and nearly every nation to this day?

Personal Reflection Questions

1. What stories do you tell yourself about the truths of the gospel (Christ's life, death, and resurrection on our behalf in order to reconcile us to the Father in heaven)?
2. Do you more often veer into doubt or faith?
3. Do you think God is surprised or disappointed in your moments of doubt?
4. What does Scripture say to those who doubt?

Prayer

Pray a prayer of confession and repentance to the Father for the ways you have meditated on doubts about Scripture. Ask the Father for the faith to believe the true story of His Son's life and work.

74. A Child of the King

———— �֍ ————

Words: Harriet E. Buell, 1834–1910
Music: John B. Sumner, 1838–1918

My Father is rich in houses and lands, He holdeth the wealth of the world in His hands! Of rubies and diamonds, of silver and gold, His coffers are full, He has riches untold. I'm a child of the King, A child of the King: With Jesus my Savior, I'm a child of the King.

My Father's own Son, the Savior of men, Once wandered on earth as the poorest of them; But now He is pleading our pardon on high, That we may be His when He comes by and by. I'm a child of the King, A child of the King: With Jesus my Savior, I'm a child of the King.

I once was an outcast stranger on earth, A sinner by choice, and an alien by birth, But I've been adopted, my name's written down, An heir to a mansion, a robe, and a crown. I'm a

child of the King, A child of the King: With Jesus my Savior,
I'm a child of the King.

Bible Study Questions

1. Read Galatians 4:1–7.
2. Who or what have been the guardians and managers set over the heir until the date set by the Father?
3. Are the children of God born children of God or made children of God?

Personal Reflection Questions

1. How do your answers above help you see more clearly your salvation as a gift from God?
2. How does this change how you speak about the gospel to others?

Prayer

Pray a prayer of adoration and worship to the Father for adopting you as one of His own, for saving you, cleansing you, and setting you apart as an heir.

75. In the Cross of Christ I Glory

———— ✠ ————

Words: John Bowring, 1792–1872
Music: Ithamar Conkey, 1815–1867

*In the cross of Christ I glory, Tow'ring o'er the wrecks of time,
All the light of sacred story Gathers round its head sublime.*

*When the woes of life o'er-take me, Hopes deceive and fears
annoy, Never shall the cross forsake me: Lo! it glows with
peace and joy.*

*When the sun of bliss is beaming Light and love upon my way,
From the cross the radiance streaming Adds new luster to the
day.*

*Bane and blessing, pain and pleasure, By the cross are sancti-
fied; Peace is there that knows no measure, Joys that thro' all
time abide.*

Bible Study Questions

1. Read Galatians 6:11–18.
2. What does it mean to boast in the cross of Christ?
3. What did Paul mean when he said he bore on his body the marks of Jesus?

Personal Reflection Questions

1. What does it mean to glory in the cross?
2. How do you glory or boast in the cross?

Prayer

Pray a prayer of thanksgiving to the Father for sending His Son into the world and for dying on the cross. Be specific about the ways the presence of the cross in the gospel causes you to worship the Lord.

76. I Heard the Voice of Jesus Say

———— ✦✦ ————

Words: Horatius Bonar, 1808–1889
Music: John B. Dykes, 1823–1876

I heard the voice of Jesus say, "Come unto Me and rest; Lay down, thou weary one, lay down Thy head upon My breast." I came to Jesus as I was, Weary, and worn, and sad; I found in Him a resting place, And He has made me glad.

I heard the voice of Jesus say, "Behold, I freely give The living water; thirsty one, Stoop down and drink, and live." I came to Jesus, and I drank Of that life-giving stream; My thirst was quench'd my soul revived, And now I live in Him.

I heard the voice of Jesus say, "I am this dark world's Light; Look unto Me, thy morn shall rise, And all thy day by bright." I looked to Jesus, and I found In Him my Star, my Sun; And in that Light of life I'll walk Till trav'ling days are done.

Bible Study Questions

1. Read Matthew 11:25–30.
2. What heavy burdens and yokes were the original hearers carrying?
3. How might the fact that Jesus said He was "meek and lowly in heart" (v. 29) have surprised the hearers?

Personal Reflection Questions

1. Which of these three stanzas most ministers to you today: that Jesus is rest, that He gives living water, or that He is light? Why?
2. In what areas of your life do you need rest, living water, or light?
3. Have you asked Him to give those things to you?

Prayer

Pray a prayer of supplication to the Father. Ask Him to provide rest for you, to give you water to quench your thirst, and to bring you into the light.

77. I Stand Amazed in the Presence

——— ✤ ———

Words: Charles H. Gabriel, 1856–1932
Music: Charles H. Gabriel, 1856–1932

I stand amazed in the presence Of Jesus the Nazarene. And wonder how He could love me, A sinner, condemned, unclean. How marvelous! how wonderful! And my song shall ever be; How marvelous! how wonderful! Is my Savior's love for me!

For me it was in the garden He prayed, "Not my will, but Thine;" He had no tears for His own griefs, But sweat drops of blood for mine. How marvelous! how wonderful! And my song shall ever be; How marvelous! how wonderful! Is my Savior's love for me!

He took my sins and my sorrows, He made them His very own; He bore the burden to Calv'ry, And suffered and died alone. How marvelous! how wonderful! And my song shall ever be; How marvelous! how wonderful! Is my Savior's love for me!

When with the ransomed in glory His face I at last shall see,
'Twill be my joy thro' the ages To sing of His love for me. How
marvelous! how wonderful! And my song shall ever be; How
marvelous! how wonderful! Is my Savior's love for me!

Bible Study Questions

1. Read Luke 22:39–46.
2. What was Jesus warning His disciples about after He found them sleeping?
3. What sort of temptation was He warning them of?

Personal Reflection Questions

1. How does knowing Christ's stance toward you is one of overwhelming love change how you live today?
2. Do you truly believe Christ is still making intercession on your behalf?
3. Do you live as though you believe that?

Prayer

Pray a prayer of confession and repentance, asking the Father to forgive you for making too little of His Son's love for you and His obedience to His Father on your behalf. Ask the Spirit for help to truly believe Christ's love for you.

78. Love Is the Theme

———— ❧ ————

Words: Albert C. Fisher, 1886–1946
Music: Albert C. Fisher, 1886–1946

Of the themes that men have known, One supremely stands alone; Thro' the ages it has shown, 'Tis His wonderful, wonderful love. Love is the theme, love is supreme; Sweeter it grows, glory bestows; Bright as the sun ever it glows! Love is the theme, eternal theme!

Let the bells of heaven ring, Let the saints their tribute bring, Let the world true praises sing For His wonderful, wonderful love. Love is the theme, love is supreme; Sweeter it grows, glory bestows; Bright as the sun ever it glows! Love is the theme, eternal theme!

Since the Lord my soul unbound, I am telling all around, Pardon, peace, and joy are found In His wonderful, wonderful love. Love is the theme, love is supreme; Sweeter it grows, glory bestows; Bright as the sun ever it glows! Love is the theme, eternal theme!

As of old when blind and lame To the blessed Master came, Sinners, call ye on His name, Trust His wonderful, wonderful love. Love is the theme, love is supreme; Sweeter it grows, glory bestows; Bright as the sun ever it glows! Love is the theme, eternal theme!

Bible Study Questions

1. Read Ephesians 3:14–21.
2. Circle all the prepositions in this passage. Try to sketch out a diagram of where all these prepositional phrases come from and lead to.

Personal Reflection Questions

1. Using your diagram from above, can you see how the love of God is tied to every piece of the gospel story?
2. If you were to omit one of these phrases (i.e., "according to the riches in his glory"), how would that change the love of God?
3. How does this encourage you in God's love today?

Prayer

Pray a prayer of adoration and worship to the Father, for loving you so wholly, so widely, so deeply. Thank Him for never forgetting you in His story and for covering all of your failures with His sacrifice and love.

79. Satisfied

———— ❧ ————

Words: Clara T. Williams, 1858–1937
Music: Ralph E. Hudon, 1843–1901

*All my life I had a longing For a drink from some clear spring,
That I hoped would quench the burning Of the thirst I felt
within. Hallelujah! I have found Him Whom my soul so long
has craved! Jesus satisfies my longing, Thro' His blood I now
am saved.*

*Feeding on the husks around me, Till my strength was almost
gone, Longed my soul for something better, Only still to hun-
ger on. Hallelujah! I have found Him Whom my soul so long
has craved! Jesus satisfies my longing, Thro' His blood I now
am saved.*

*Poor I was, and sought for riches, Something that would sat-
isfy, But the dust I gathered round me Only mocked my soul's
sad cry. Hallelujah! I have found Him Whom my soul so long*

has craved! Jesus satisfies my longing, Thro' His blood I now am saved.

Well of water, ever springing, Bread of life so rich and free, Untold wealth that never falleth, My Redeemer is to me. Hallelujah! I have found Him Whom my soul so long has craved! Jesus satisfies my longing, Thro' His blood I now am saved.

Bible Study Questions

1. Read John 4:1–30.
2. Why was this woman coming to the well at noontime, the hottest part of the day?
3. Why did the disciples marvel that Jesus was talking with a woman?

Personal Reflection Questions

1. Are there places in your life that never feel satisfied by the living water of Christ?
2. Do you attempt to hide those places or pretend they don't exist? Why or why not?
3. What does the living water of Christ satisfy in you today?

Prayer

Pray a prayer of thanksgiving to the Father for sending His Son to bring living water to all your most parched places. Ask Him to satisfy you today with the truth of Scripture and the gospel.

80. I Will Sing the Wondrous Story

———— �֍ ————

Words: Francis H. Rowley, 1854–1952
Music: Peter P. Bilhorn, 1865–1936

*I will sing the wondrous story Of the Christ who died for me,
How He left His home in glory For the cross of Calvary. Yes,
I'll sing the wondrous story, Of the Christ who died for me,
Sing it with the saints in glory, Gathered by the crystal sea.*

*I was lost, but Jesus found me, Found the sheep that went
astray, Threw His loving arms around me, Drew me back into
His way. Yes, I'll sing the wondrous story, Of the Christ who
died for me, Sing it with the saints in glory, Gathered by the
crystal sea.*

*I was bruised, but Jesus healed me; Faint was I from many a
fall; Sight was gone, and fears possessed me, But He freed me
from them all. Yes, I'll sing the wondrous story, Of the Christ
who died for me, Sing it with the saints in glory, Gathered by
the crystal sea.*

Days of darkness still come o'er me, Sorrow's paths I often tread, But the Savior still is with me; By His hand I'm safely led. Yes, I'll sing the wondrous story, Of the Christ who died for me, Sing it with the saints in glory, Gathered by the crystal sea.

He will keep me till the river Rolls its waters at my feet. Then He'll bear me safely over, Where the loved ones I shall meet. Yes, I'll sing the wondrous story, Of the Christ who died for me, Sing it with the saints in glory, Gathered by the crystal sea.

Bible Study Questions

1. Read Matthew 18:10–14.
2. Now read all of Matthew 18. What do you think is the significance of placing the above passage in there?
3. How do you read it differently within its context?

Personal Reflection Questions

1. Think of a time when the Spirit of God wouldn't let you go.
2. Did you feel found out or cared for by Him in that time?
3. Write out a testimony of how the Good Shepherd came after you and share it with someone.

Prayer

Pray a prayer of thanksgiving to the Father for sending His Son to rescue and redeem you for His purposes. Worship Him for His goodness and faithfulness to you.

81. Forever with the Lord

———— ✤ ————

Words: James Montgomery, 1771–1854
Music: Franklin L. Sheppard, 1852–1930

"Forever with the Lord!" Amen, so let it be! Life from His death is in the word, 'Tis immortality. My Father's house on high, Home of my soul, how near At times to faith's forseeing eye The golden streets appear!

"Forever with the Lord!" Forever in His will, The promise of that faithful word, Lord, here in me fulfill. With you at my right hand, Then I shall never fail; Uphold me, Lord, and I shall stand; Thro' grace I will prevail.

So when my latest breath Breaks thro' the veil of pain, By death I shall escape from death, And life eternal gain. That resurrection word, That shout of victory: One more, "Forever with the Lord!" Amen, so let it be!

Bible Study Questions

1. Read Matthew 19:16–30.
2. Why did the rich, young ruler turn away sorrowful? What did he not want to lose?
3. Search the Scriptures to find what is promised to those who lose their possessions or even their life on earth for the sake of Christ.

Personal Reflection Questions

1. What do you fear losing? Why?
2. What would happen if you were to lose any of these things (house, car, family, money, job, respect, etc.)?
3. What might the Spirit be asking you to relinquish today?

Prayer

Pray a prayer of confession and repentance for placing a higher value on the gifts than you place on the Giver of all good gifts. Ask the Spirit for help in rightly ordering what you have been given.

82. My Savior First of All

———— ✤ ————

Words: Fanny J. Crosby, 1820–1915
Music: John R. Sweney, 1837–1899

*When my lifework is ended, and I cross the swelling tide,
When the bright and glorious morning I shall see; I shall know
my Redeemer when I reach the other side, And His smile will
be the first to welcome me. I shall know Him, I shall know
Him, And redeemed by His side I shall stand. I shall know
Him, I shall know Him By the print of the nails in His hand.*

*Oh, the soul-thrilling rapture when I view His blessed face,
And the luster of His kindly beaming eye; How my full heart
will praise Him for the mercy, love, and grace That prepared
for me a mansion in the sky. I shall know Him, I shall know
Him, And redeemed by His side I shall stand. I shall know
Him, I shall know Him By the print of the nails in His hand.*

*Oh, the dear ones in glory, how they beckon me to come, And
our parting at the river I recall; To the sweet vales of Eden*

they will sing my welcome home, But I long to meet my Savior first of all. I shall know Him, I shall know Him, And redeemed by His side I shall stand. I shall know Him, I shall know Him By the print of the nails in His hand.

Thro' the gates to the city in a robe of spotless white, He will lead me where no tears will ever fall; In the glad song of ages I shall mingle with delight, But I long to meet my Savior first of all. I shall know Him, I shall know Him, And redeemed by His side I shall stand. I shall know Him, I shall know Him By the print of the nails in His hand.

Bible Study Questions

1. Read Revelation 1:4–20.
2. What do you think the keys to death and hell are?
3. Why do you think John gave his readers this description of the Son of Man?

Personal Reflection Questions

1. When you envision meeting Jesus for the first time, what do you imagine that moment to be like?
2. Will you be relieved? Ashamed? Fearful? In awe?
3. Why?

Prayer

Pray a prayer of worship to the Father for His good and gracious plan of redemption, and for the certainty of all God's children of meeting Christ face-and-face and spending eternity with Him.

83. Jerusalem, the Golden

———— ✢ ————

Words: Bernard of Cluny, 12th Century; tr. John Mason Neale,
    1818–1866
Music: Alexander C. Ewing, 1830–1895

Jerusalem, the golden, With milk and honey blest! Beneath thy contemplation Sink heart and voice oppressed; I know not, O I know not What joys await me there; What radiancy of glory, What bliss beyond compare.

They stand, those halls of Zion, All jubilant with song, And bright with many angels, And all the martyr throng; The Prince is ever in them, The daylight is serene; The pastures of the blessed Are decked in glorious sheen.

O sweet and blessed country, Shall I e'er see thy face? O sweet and blessed country, Shall I e'er win thy grace? Exult, O dust and ashes! The Lord shall be thy part; His only, His forever, Thou shalt be, and thou art!

Bible Study Questions

1. Read Hebrews 11.
2. What is the "better" that keeps occurring in this passage?
3. Will the men and women in this passage ever see the "better"?

Personal Reflection Questions

1. Do you view the new heaven and new earth with expectation?
2. Is it easier for you to get caught up in today's circumstances or in the hope of the future with Christ?
3. How might today look different if you desired "a better country"?

Prayer

Pray a prayer of thanksgiving that the Father has prepared a place for you and for all His children. Ask the Spirit for help as you walk through your days on earth, living in the hope and expectation of eternity.

84. We're Marching to Zion

———— ✤✤ ————

Words: Isaac Watts, 1674–1748
Music: Robert Lowry, 1826–1899

Come, we that love the Lord, And let our joys be known; Join in a song with sweet accord, Join in a long with sweet accord, And thus surround the throne, And thus surround the throne. We're marching to Zion, Beautiful, beautiful Zion; We're marching upward to Zion, The beautiful city of God.

Let those refuse to sing Who never knew our God; But children of the heav'nly King, But children of the heav'nly King, May speak their joys abroad, May speak their joys abroad. We're marching to Zion, Beautiful, beautiful Zion; We're marching upward to Zion, The beautiful city of God.

The hill of Zion yields A thousand sacred sweets, Before we reach the heav'nly fields, Before we reach the heav'nly fields, Or walk the golden streets, Or walk the golden streets. We're marching to Zion, Beautiful, beautiful Zion; We're marching upward to Zion, The beautiful city of God.

Then let our songs abound, And ev'ry tear be dry; we're marching thro' Immanuel's ground, We're marching thro' Immanuel's ground, To fairer worlds on high, To fairer worlds on high. We're marching to Zion, Beautiful, beautiful Zion; We're marching upward to Zion, The beautiful city of God.

Bible Study Questions

1. Read Revelation 21.
2. Why do you think this passage is so specific in its description of the new city?
3. Are those precious jewels, gold, and silver there to make those who abide there feel rich, or are they there to say something about the place itself?

Personal Reflection Questions

1. Do you look forward to the new heaven and new earth mainly because of what you get there or because of Who you will encounter there? Why?

2. What are some aspects of this broken and incomplete world that you look forward to not being a part of in the new heaven and new earth?

3. How might Christ be asking you to advance His kingdom on earth as it is now?

Prayer

Pray a prayer of supplication to the Father. Ask Him to advance the kingdom of God quickly on earth.

85. When the Morning Comes

———— ❧ ————

Words: Charles A. Tindley, 1851–1933; alt. and arr. B. B.
     McKinney, 1886–1952
Music: Charles A. Tindley, 1851–1933; alt. and arr. B. B.
     McKinney, 1886–1952

Trials dark on ev'ry hand, and we cannot understand All the ways that God would lead us to that blessed promised land; But He'll guide us with His eye, and we'll follow till we die; We will understand it better by and by, when the morning comes, When the saints of God are gathered home, We will tell the story how we've overcome; We will understand it better by and by.

Oft our cherished plans have failed, disappointments have prevailed, And we've wandered in the darkness, heavy-hearted and alone; But we're trusting in the Lord, and, according to His Word, We will understand it better by and by, when the morning comes, When the saints of God are gathered home,

We will tell the story how we've overcome; We will understand it better by and by.

Temptations, hidden snares often take us unawares, And our hearts are made to bleed for some tho'tless word or deed, And we wonder why the test when we try to do our best, Bet we'll understand it better by and by, when the morning comes, When the saints of God are gathered home, We will tell the story how we've overcome; We will understand it better by and by.

Bible Study Questions

1. Read Psalm 30.
2. Make a list of what man does in this passage (i.e., "I cried unto thee."). List what God does (i.e., "Thou hast healed me.").

Personal Reflection Questions

1. Using your list from above, think about the last time you cried out for help, sang praises to the Lord, rebelled in your prosperity, etc.
2. Think about God's response to you in those moments.

Prayer

Pray a pray of worship and praise, thanking God for His attentiveness to you, even in your misery and rebellion. Thank Him for a future forever with Him, where no evil or tears exist.

86. O That Will Be Glory

———— ✿ ————

Words: Charles H. Gabriel, 1856–1932
Music: Charles H. Gabriel, 1856–1932

When all my labors and trials are o'er, And I am safe on that beautiful shore, Just to be near the dear Lord I adore, Will thro' the ages be glory for me. O that will be glory for me, Glory for me, glory for me, When by His grace I shall look on His face, That will be glory, be glory for me.

When, by the gift of His infinite grace, I am accorded in heaven a place, Just to be there and to look on His face, Will thro' the ages be glory for me. O that will be glory for me, Glory for me, glory for me, When by His grace I shall look on His face, That will be glory, be glory for me.

Friends will be there I have loved long ago; Joy like a river around me will flow; Yet just a smile from me Savior, I know, Will thro' the ages be glory for me. O that will be glory for me,

Glory for me, glory for me, When by His grace I shall look on His face, That will be glory, be glory for me.

Bible Study Questions

1. Read Jude 24.
2. Who keeps you from stumbling?
3. Who presents you blameless?
4. Whose glory and whose joy is it for?

Personal Reflection Questions

1. Do you often feel like you have to keep yourself from stumbling or remaining blameless?
2. Do you do this for your own glory or for God's?
3. What would it look like to trust the Lord to keep you from stumbling and doing it for glory alone?

Prayer

Pray a prayer of confession and repentance for trying to manage your own sin, weaknesses, and life. Ask the Spirit for help in self-forgetfulness, for God's glory alone.

87. Shall We Gather at the River

––––––– ✤ –––––––

Words: Robert Lowry, 1826–1899
Music: Robert Lowry, 1826–1899

Shall we gather at the river, Where bright angel feet have trod; With its crystal tide forever Flowing by the throne of God? Yes, we'll gather at the river, The beautiful, the beautiful river; Gather with the saints at the river That flows by the throne of God.

On the margin of the river, Washing up its silver spray, We will walk and worship ever, All the happy golden day. Yes, we'll gather at the river, The beautiful, the beautiful river; Gather with the saints at the river That flows by the throne of God.

Ere we reach the shining river, Lay we ev'ry burden down; Grace our spirits will deliver, And provide a robe and crown. Yes, we'll gather at the river, The beautiful, the beautiful river; Gather with the saints at the river That flows by the throne of God.

Soon we'll reach the shining river, Soon our pilgrimage will cease; Soon our happy hearts will quiver With the melody of peace. Yes, we'll gather at the river, The beautiful, the beautiful river; Gather with the saints at the river That flows by the throne of God.

Bible Study Questions

1. Read Psalm 46.
2. How can streams make the city of God glad?
3. What was the poet trying to help his hearers understand about the river of God?

Personal Reflection Questions

1. Do you think of the new heaven and new earth as a real place with real mountains, rivers, lakes, and people? Why or why not?
2. What do you envision when you think of the new heaven and new earth?
3. How is this consistent with Scripture?

Prayer

Pray a prayer of supplication to the Father, asking Him to reveal to you through Scripture what His plan for eternity is. Ask Him to enlarge your concept of the new heaven and new earth.

88. Joy to the World!
The Lord Is Come

—— ❈ ——

Words: Isaac Watts, 1674-1748
Music: George Frederick Handel, 1685–1759; arr. Lowell Mason,
    1792–1872

*Joy to the world! the Lord is come; Let earth receive her King;
Let ev'ry heart prepare Him room, And heav'n and nature
sing, And heav'n and nature sing, And heav'n, and heav'n and
nature sing.*

*Joy to the earth! the Savior reigns; Let men their songs
employ; While fields and floods, rocks, hills, and plains Repeat
the sounding joy, Repeat the sounding joy, Repeat, repeat the
sounding joy.*

*No more let sins and sorrows grow, Nor thorns infest the
ground; He comes to make His blessings flow Far as the curse
is found, Far as the curse is found, Far as, far as the curse is
found.*

He rules the world with truth and grace, And makes the nations prove The glories of His righteousness, And wonders of His love, And wonders of His love, And wonders, wonders of His love.

Bible Study Questions

1. Read Psalm 98.
2. What words are used to describe the "noise" that you are called to make toward God?
3. Find three places in Scripture that describe how one would prepare to receive a king.

Personal Reflection Questions

1. List out the blessings that God has flowed into your life.
2. Write out your new song unto the Lord. Don't worry about it making it into the hymnal; write from your heart.
3. What is a place in your life that you need to prepare for your King's coming?

Prayer

Lord, I praise You for Your blessings that You have poured out over my life. I praise You for Your provision. I know that no matter how much I have prepared, my life will never be clean enough to receive You, and I thank You for Your mercy and forgiveness. I know that no matter what I do, nothing is strong enough to pull me away from Your hand. Give me the words to express my heart's desires.

89. Hark! The Herald Angels Sing

———— ✤ ————

Words: Charles Wesley, 1707–1788, alt. George Whitefield,
    1714–1770
Music: Felix Mendelssohn, 1809–1847; arr. William H.
    Cummings, 1831–1915

Hark! the herald angels sing, "Glory to the newborn King;
Peace on earth, and mercy mild; God and sinners reconciled."
Joyful, all ye nations, rise, Join the triumph of the skies; With
angelic hosts proclaim, "Christ is born in Bethlehem!" Hark!
he herald angels sing, "Glory to the new-born King."

Christ, by highest heav'n adored, Christ, the everlasting Lord:
Late in time, behold Him come, Off-spring of a virgin's womb.
Veiled in flesh the God-head see, Hail th'incarnate Deity!
Pleased as man with men to dwell, Jesus our Immanuel. Hark!
the herald angels sing, "Glory to the new-born King."

Hail the heav'n born Prince of Peace! Hail the Sun of righ-
teousness! Light and life to all He brings, Ris'n with healing

in His wings. Mild He lays His glory by, Born that man no more may die, Born to raise the sons of earth, Born to give them second birth. Hark! the herald angels sing, "Glory to the new-born King."

Bible Study Questions

1. Read Luke 2. How are the angels involved in the story and what parts do they play?

2. Explain in your own words how God and sinners have been reconciled.

3. Can you think of another place in Scripture where the angels sing praises around Jesus? What are the words of their song then?

Personal Reflection Questions

1. Reflect on each phrase of the last verse: "Mild He lays His glory by, Born that man no more may die, Born to raise the sons of earth, Born to give them second birth. Hark! the herald angels sing, 'Glory to the new-born King'." How do each of these phrases differ?

2. Rewrite all three verses in your own words. Say them out loud to God. Do you believe what you are saying?

3. What "light and life" has Jesus brought into your life?

Prayer

Father, You sent Your one and only Son to earth to save us all from our own sin. I cannot fathom that much love. Help me bring glory to Jesus with my life. Help me to never forget the sacrifice He made. It was not just on the cross at the end of His earthly life, but when He set aside His crown, to come to earth as a baby. May my joy be so great and evident, that all who are around me would praise Your name.

90. O Come, All Ye Faithful

——— ❈ ———

Words: Latin hymn; ascribed to John Francis Wade, c. 1710–
1786; tr. Frederick Oakley, 1802–1880 and others
Music: John Francis Wade, c. 1710–1786

*O come, all ye faithful, joyful and triumphant, O come ye, O
come ye to Bethlehem! Come and behold Him, born the King
of angels! O come, let us adore Him, O come, let us adore Him,
O come, let us adore Him, Christ the Lord!*

*Sing, choirs of angels, sing in exultation, O sing, all ye bright
hosts of heav'n avove! Glory to God, all glory in the highest!
O come, let us adore Him, O come, let us adore Him, O come,
let us adore Him, Christ the Lord!*

*Yes, Lord, we greet Thee, born his happy morning, Jesus,
to Thee be all glory giv'n; Word of the Father, now in flesh
appearing! O come, let us adore Him, O come, let us adore
Him, O come, let us adore Him, Christ the Lord!*

Bible Study Questions

1. Read Luke 2. List out all the people involved in the story and how they showed their adoration for the Lord.

2. Read Deuteronomy 11:1. Write out the ways listed in this verse to adore God.

3. Explain in your own words, using Scripture reference, "Word of the Father, now in flesh appearing."

Personal Reflection Questions

1. How do you show your adoration for the Lord?

2. When was the last time that you sat in silent adoration of God? Take 5 minutes now in silent adoration.

3. Write about a time when God left you in a place of awe.

Prayer

All I want Lord is to be counted among the faithful. Help me to follow You in all I do. Lord, allow me to be called into Your presence. Let me stand in Your glory and praise Your name. Teach me when to be still and silent, and when to praise You with my voice.

REFLECT *on*
THE ENTIRE SERIES

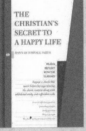

978-1-4336-4999-8   978-1-4336-4996-7   978-1-4336-5003-1   978-1-4336-4993-6

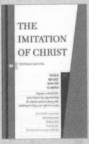

978-1-4627-4766-5   978-1-4627-4768-9   978-1-4627-4763-4